C000135825

CHAMONIX TO ZERMATT
'The Walker's Haute Route'

About the Author

Kev Reynolds is a freelance writer, photojournalist and lecturer whose first title for Cicerone Press (*Walks & Climbs in the Pyrenees*) appeared in 1978, and is still in print. He has published many books on the Alps, a series of trekkers' guides to the Nepal Himalaya and, nearer to home, several on walking in southern England. He has walked, trekked and/or climbed in many European mountain ranges, as well as in North Africa, South America and the Himalaya. A number of his most memorable experiences in these mountains have been published by Cicerone in *A Walk in the Clouds*.

The first Honorary Member of the BAEML (now the British Association of International Mountain Leaders) and a member of the Alpine Club, Austrian Alpine Club and Outdoor Writers and Photographers Guild, Kev's enthusiasm for mountains in particular, and the countryside in general, remains undiminished after more than 50 years of activity. Living among what he calls the 'Kentish Alps' he regularly travels throughout Britain to share that enthusiasm through his lectures. Check him out on www.kevreynolds.co.uk.

Other Cicerone guides by the author

100 Hut Walks in the Alps	*Tour of the Jungfrau Region*
A Walk in the Clouds	*Tour of the Oisans: The GR54*
Alpine Pass Route	*Tour of the Vanoise*
Alpine Points of View	*Trekking in the Alps*
Central Switzerland	*Trekking in the Himalaya*
Ecrins National Park	*Trekking in the Silvretta and*
Everest: A Trekker's Guide	*Rätikon Alps*
Langtang with Gosainkund and	*Walking in Austria*
Helambu: A Trekker's Guide	*Walking in Kent*
Manaslu: A Trekker's Guide	*Walking in Sussex*
The Bernese Alps – Switzerland	*Walking in the Alps*
The Cotswold Way	*Walking in the Valais*
The North Downs Way	*Walking in Ticino – Switzerland*
The Pyrenees	*Walks and Climbs in the Pyrenees*
The South Downs Way	*Walks in the Engadine – Switzerland*
The Swiss Alps	*Walks in the South Downs*
Tour of Mont Blanc	*National Park*

CHAMONIX TO ZERMATT

'The Walker's Haute Route'

by

Kev Reynolds

2 POLICE SQUARE, MILNTHORPE, CUMBRIA LA7 7PY
www.cicerone.co.uk

Printed in China on behalf of Latitude Press Ltd.
A catalogue record for this book is available from the British Library.

*For my wife – without whose love and practical support
this guidebook would not have been written.*

ACKNOWLEDGEMENTS

During research for this latest edition I was the beneficiary of much kindness, hospitality and generous friendship, and wish to publicly thank Bob Gibbons and Sîan Pritchard-Jones for emergency assistance; Lise Cachat at the Pension En Plein Air in Champex; Urbain Troukens and Mirielle Budts at Pension du Lac Bleu in La Gouille; Olivier and Valérie Demange, guardians at Cabane Bella Tola; my good friends Hedy Füx-Pollinger at Jungen; and Peter Pollinger at Hotel La Réserve in St Niklaus – all of whom helped to make this a truly memorable trek. Marcelline Kuonen at Switzerland Travel in London gave welcome assistance in advance, and I'm grateful, too, to the many readers of previous editions of this guide who wrote with updates and recommendations, among them: Nick Aitchison, Christy Alvord, David Angell, Andrew Archibald, Chris Barnes, Tom Boudreau, Geoff Brelsford, John Castle, Richard and Elaine Clare, Tim Ford, Mike Fry, Paul Gittins, R Glaister, Frank Gordon, Nigel Greenwood, Charles Hewlings, David Hughes, Ron King, Daniel Kligler, Tim Lamont-Smith, Peter Lewis, Jolanda and Marcel Locher, Jenny Morgan, Liz Nicholas, Phil Nixon, David and Jenny Norgrove, John Owen, Jane Linz Roberts, Graeme Rogers, Ron Roweth, Hilary Sharp, John Simpson, David Slater, Tania Smith, David Whewell, Nick Wilkie, Bill Williams and Holly Gorton, Peter Wilson and Christian Wulff, with apologies to any left out whose names I could not decipher. I am grateful to Jonathan and Lesley Williams who checked the route for me in 2010 while I was working on another guide. A special word of thanks to my old trekking partner Alan Payne for his company when we first worked out the route all those years ago, and to my wife who has now trekked it with me twice. And finally, I am thankful as ever for the continued backing of Jonathan Williams at Cicerone who provides so many excuses to spend long weeks in the Alps and elsewhere, and to the whole Cicerone team whose skills and talents are put to my benefit. My sincere thanks to them all.

Kev Reynolds

Front cover: High above Zermatt the trail passes through Tufteren (Stage 14)

CONTENTS

Updates to this Guide

While every effort is made by our authors to ensure the accuracy of guidebooks as they go to print, changes can occur during the lifetime of an edition. Any updates that we know of for this guide will be on the Cicerone website (www.cicerone.co.uk/780/updates), so please check before planning your trip. We also advise that you check information about such things as transport, accommodation and shops locally. Even rights of way can be altered over time. We are always grateful for information about any discrepancies between a guidebook and the facts on the ground, sent by email to info@cicerone.co.uk or by post to Cicerone, 2 Police Square, Milnthorpe LA7 7PY, United Kingdom.

Mountain Safety

Every mountain walk has its dangers, and those described in this guidebook are no exception. All who walk or climb in the mountains should recognise this and take responsibility for themselves and their companions along the way. The author and publisher have made every effort to ensure that the information contained in this guide was correct when it went to press, but they cannot accept responsibility for any loss, injury or inconvenience sustained by any person using this book.

International Distress Signal *(emergency only)*
Six blasts on a whistle (and flashes with a torch after dark) spaced evenly for one minute, followed by a minute's pause. Repeat until an answer is received. The response is three signals per minute followed by a minute's pause.

Helicopter Rescue
The following signals are used to communicate with a helicopter:

Help needed:
raise both arms
above head to
form a 'Y'

Help not needed:
raise one arm
above head, extend
other arm downward

Emergency telephone numbers
France: PGHM (Peloton de Gendarmerie de Haute Montagne):
☎ 04 50 53 16 89; Emergency services: ☎ 112 (mobile phones)
Switzerland: OCVS (Organisation Cantonale Valaisanne de Secours): ☎144

Weather reports
(If telephoning from the UK the dialling codes are:
France: 0033; Switzerland: 0041

France: www.meteo.fr or ☎ 3250
Switzerland: ☎ 162 (in French, German or Italian), www.meteoschweiz.ch/en

Note Mountain rescue can be very expensive – be adequately insured.

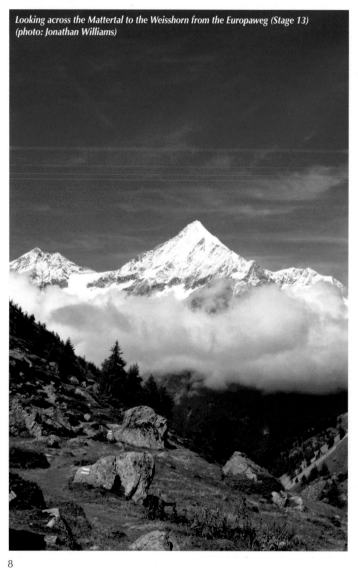

Looking across the Mattertal to the Weisshorn from the Europaweg (Stage 13) (photo: Jonathan Williams)

Map key

═══════════	road
··················	main route
··················	alt route
··················	alt route
▬·▬·▬·▬·▬	national boundary
～～～～	ridge
⊢─────⊣	cablecar
～～～～	river
	lake
	glacier
●	town
▲	summit
⋊⋉	col
⬆	refuge
⨇	camp
⁂	forest
✝●	church

Profile key

⬆	refuge
⏅	refreshment
⨇	camp
🚐	bus
🚎	tram
⬛	cablecar

9

Chamonix to Zermatt

Crans
Montana

Turtmann

Brig

Sierre

Bella Tola
3025m

SWITZERLAND

VAL D'ANNIVIERS

TURTMANNTAL

Visp

St
Niklaus

Grächen

Gasenried

Gruben

Grimentz

VAL D'HÉRENS

Zinal

Barrhorn
3610m

Riedgletscher

Saas Fee

Evolène

Come de Sorebois
2895m

Turtmanngletscher

La Sage

Glacier
de Moiry

Weisshorn
4506m

Dom
4545m

Bauderes

Zinalrothorn
4221m

Taschhorn
4491m

MATTERTAL

Arolla

Ober
Gabelhorn

Dent Blanche
4358m

Zermatt

Stellihorn
3436m

Pigne
d'Arolla
3796m

Glacier
du Mont
Mine

Tête
Blanche

Findelgletscher

...m

...de
...on

Mont
Collon
3637m

Matterhorn
4478m

Gomergletscher

...acier
...emma

Theodulgletscher

Liskamm
4479m

Monte Rosa
Dufourspitze
4634m

Becca di Luseney
3504m

ITALY

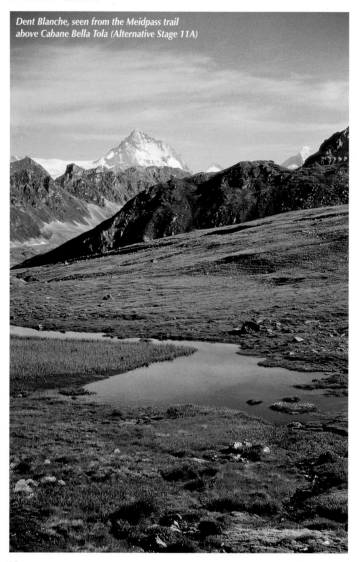

Dent Blanche, seen from the Meidpass trail above Cabane Bella Tola (Alternative Stage 11A)

PREFACE TO THE FIFTH EDITION

Research for this new edition was carried out in the summer of 2013, and reflects several, mostly minor, changes to the route described in earlier editions. A few of these changes are man-made, but some occur as a result of global warming that has increased the risk of both rockfall and landslide. I have also taken the opportunity to include more details of accommodation along the way, in the light not only of personal experience, but thanks to the recommendation of readers.

What has not changed in the decade and a half since this guide was first published is the beauty of the mountains and the charm of the valleys. Glaciers may shrivel, rockfall rearrange a section of hillside, lakes grow in extent or shrink around their edges, but the scenic rewards of the Chamonix to Zermatt Walker's Haute Route are every bit as powerful as they ever were. It's a fabulous route across an amazing series of landscapes.

May your journey along it be as rewarding and memorable as each of mine has been.

Kev Reynolds, 2015

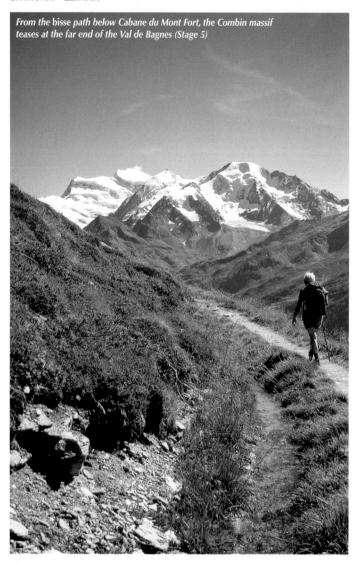

From the bisse path below Cabane du Mont Fort, the Combin massif teases at the far end of the Val de Bagnes (Stage 5)

INTRODUCTION

Chamonix to Zermatt, Mont Blanc to the Matterhorn. What pictures these names conjure in the minds of those of us who love mountains! The two greatest mountaineering centres in the world – one overshadowed by the highest massif in Western Europe and the other by the most famous, if not the most elegant and most instantly recognised, of all mountains.

Chamonix to Zermatt, Mont Blanc to the Matterhorn – recipe for a visual feast!

To walk from one to the other is to sample that feast in full measure; a gourmet extravaganza of scenic wonders from first day till last, and each one (to carry the metaphor to its limit) a course that both satisfies and teases the palate for more.

The Walker's Haute Route does just that.

In two weeks of mountain travel you will be witness to the greatest collection of 4000m peaks in all the Alps and visit some of the most spectacular valleys. There you'll find delightful villages and remote alp hamlets, wander flower meadows and deep fragrant forests, skirt exquisite tarns that toss mountains on their heads, cross icy streams and clamber beside glaciers that hang suspended from huge buttresses of rock. You'll traverse lonely passes and descend into wild, stone-filled corries. There will be marmots among the boulders and ibex on the heights. And your days will be filled with wonder.

It's more demanding than the well-known Tour du Mont Blanc, for the route is over 180km long; it crosses eleven passes, gains more than 12,000m in height and loses more than 10,000m. But each pass gained is a window onto a world of stunning beauty.

There's the Mont Blanc range and the chain of the Pennine Alps, one massif after another of snow-bound glory: Mont Blanc itself, with its organ-pipe aiguilles; the overpowering mass of the Grand Combin; Mont Blanc de Cheilon and Pigne d'Arolla, Mont Collon and Tête Blanche and the huge tooth of Dent Blanche. There's the Grand Cornier, Ober Gabelhorn and Weisshorn and stiletto-pointed Zinalrothorn; then there's the Dom and Täschhorn, Breithorn and Matterhorn and all their crowding neighbours sheathed in ice and snow to act as a backcloth to dreams; a background landscape to the Walker's Haute Route, contender for the title of Most Beautiful Walk in Europe.

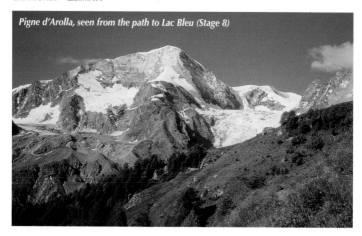

Pigne d'Arolla, seen from the path to Lac Bleu (Stage 8)

THE WALKER'S HAUTE ROUTE

The original High Level Route (*Haute Route*), from Chamonix to Zermatt and beyond, was developed more than a hundred years ago. But this was very much a mountaineer's expedition, for it traced a meandering line among the great peaks of the Pennine Alps by linking a number of glacier passes. James David Forbes, scientist and active mountaineer, pioneered an important section of this in 1842 when he crossed Col d'Hérens, Col de Fenêtre and Col du Mont Collon. Alfred Wills also made early explorations, but it was mainly a joint effort by other members of the Alpine Club, notably JF Hardy, William Mathews,

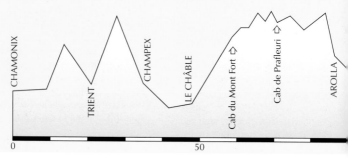

THE WALKER'S HAUTE ROUTE

CHAMONIX

TRIENT

CHAMPEX

LE CHÂBLE

Cab du Mont Fort ⇧

Cab de Prafleuri ⇧

AROLLA

0　　　　　　　　　　　　50

Francis Fox Tuckett, FW Jacomb and Stephen Winkworth and their guides, that saw a complete High Level Route established in 1861. This route went from Chamonix to Col d'Argentière, then via Val Ferret, Orsières, Bourg St Pierre, Col de Sonadon, Col d'Oren, Praraye, Col de Valpelline and on to Zermatt.

The following year (1862) Col des Planards was discovered, which led to Orsières being by-passed, thereby allowing a better line to be made in the link between the northern edge of the Mont Blanc range and that of the Pennine Alps.

This High Level Route was, of course, primarily a summer mountaineering expedition that was no small undertaking, especially when one considers the fact that at the time there were no mountain huts as we know them now and all supplies had to be carried a very long way. But with the introduction of skis to the Alps in the late 19th century a

new concept in winter travel became apparent, and with the first important ski tour being made in the Bernese Alps in 1897, and the subsequent winter ascent of major mountains aided by ski (Monte Rosa in 1898, Breithorn 1899, Strahlhorn 1901, etc), it was clearly only a matter of time before the challenge of the High Level Route would be subjected to winter assault.

In 1903 the first attempt was made to create a ski traverse of the Pennine Alps, and although this and other attempts failed, in January 1911 Roget, Kurz, Murisier, the brothers Crettex and Louis Theytaz succeeded in establishing a winter route from Bourg St Pierre to Zermatt.

Having successfully hijacked the original High Level Route as the ski-touring route *par excellence*, and having translated its British title as the Haute Route, the journey from Chamonix to Zermatt came to be seen almost universally as a winter

Val de Moiry headwall, seen from the Alpage de Torrent (Alternative Stage 9)

(or more properly, a spring) expedition; a true classic that is, understandably, the focus of ambition for many experienced skiers and ski-mountaineers today.

But there's another Chamonix to Zermatt high level route that is very much a classic of its kind; a walker's route that never quite reaches 3000m on any of its passes, that requires no technical mountaineering skills to achieve, avoids glacier crossings and yet rewards with some of the most dramatic high mountain views imaginable.

This is the Chamonix to Zermatt Walker's Haute Route.

It leads comfortably from the base of Mont Blanc to the Swiss frontier at Col de Balme, and from there down to Trient following the route of the Tour of Mont Blanc or one of its *variantes*. The next pass is Fenêtre d'Arpette leading to Champex, and

from there down to the junction of Val d'Entremont and Val de Bagnes, then curving round the foot of the mountains to Le Châble. Avoiding Verbier, a steep climb brings you to Cabane du Mont Fort, and continues high above the valley heading south-east before crossing three cols in quick succession in order to pass round the northern flanks of Rosablanche.

From Cabane de Prafleuri the route heads over Col des Roux and along the shores of Lac des Dix, then on to Arolla by one of two ways: Col de Riedmatten or the neighbouring Pas de Chèvres via Cabane des Dix. Arolla leads to Les Haudères and up to La Sage on a green hillside above Val d'Hérens in readiness for tackling either Col de Torrent or Col du Tsaté. Both these cols give access to Val de Moiry and its hut perched in full view of a tremendous icefall, from where the crossing of Col de Sorebois takes the walker into Val de Zinal, the upper reaches of the glorious Val d'Anniviers. From Zinal to Gruben in the Turtmanntal the route once again has two options to consider: either by way of Hotel Weisshorn or Cabane Bella Tola and the Meidpass, or by the more direct Forcletta. After leaving Gruben a final climb to the ancient crossing point of the Augstbordpass leads to the Mattertal. A long but easy valley walk to Zermatt is the basic final stage, but a two-day alternative and much better option (if it is safe and open) adopts the dramatic Europaweg which makes a true high-level traverse of the east wall of the valley, with an overnight stay in the Europa Hut.

Every stage has its own special attributes, its own unique splendour, and all add up to a walk of classic proportions. It is, of course, a scenic extravaganza whose main features are the mountains that form the landscapes through which you walk.

First of these is dominated by the Mont Blanc massif with its towering aiguilles creating stark outlines against a backwash of snow and ice. Unbelievably high and seemingly remote from valley-based existence, the dome of the Monarch of the Alps glows of an evening, shines under a midday sun and imposes itself on panoramas viewed from cols several days' walk from the crowded boulevards of Chamonix.

Then there's the Grand Combin making a fair imitation of its loftier neighbour as it soars above the deeply cut Val de Bagnes. This too is a vast mountain whose presence is felt many days' walk away, a grand block of glacial artistry that lures and entices from afar.

Heading round Rosablanche gives a taste of the other side of the mountain world, where gaunt screes and dying glaciers contrast the gleaming snows of its upper slopes. But then Mont Blanc de Cheilon returns the eye to grandeur on an epic scale, with Pigne d'Arolla and Mont Collon adding their handsome profiles for close inspection, while far off a first brief glimpse of the Matterhorn promises much for the future.

Val de Moiry holds many surprises with its tarns, dammed lake, majestic icefall and contorted glaciers, while Col de Sorebois and all the way down to Zinal is one long adoration of the Weisshorn. The head of Val de Zinal is so magnificent that one yearns to be able to explore further, but the route northward denies that opportunity yet still allows it to be seen in true perspective – a fabulous cirque giving birth to glaciers that have carved a valley of much loveliness.

The Turtmanntal takes you back to the nineteenth century. Above it once more rises the Weisshorn, along with Tête de Milon, Bishorn and Brunegghorn and a caliper of glaciers spilling into the valley.

One of the finest viewpoints of the whole walk comes an hour and a half below the Augstbordpass between Turtmanntal and Mattertal.

The Mattertal is a long green shaft 1000m below. Across the valley shines the Dom with the tongue-like Riedgletscher hanging from it. Above to the right is the Brunegghorn with the Weisshorn beyond, while at the head of the valley is seen that great snowy mass which runs between Monte Rosa and the Matterhorn. But the Matterhorn itself keeps you waiting. Cross the valley at St Niklaus and climb steeply to Gasenried, then walk the length of the Europaweg and you'll not only have the Bishorn and Weisshorn (yet again), but also the Schalihorn, Pointe Sud de Moming and Zinalrothorn, and the incomparable Matterhorn at last seen as it should be seen, from its roots above Zermatt to its cocked-head summit

nearly 3000m above the valley. It's a view worth waiting for. A view worth walking all the way from Chamonix to savour.

Despite its high passes, despite the fact that it runs across the grain of the country where deep valleys slice between the long outstretched arms of some of the highest mountains in Western Europe, the Chamonix to Zermatt route is not the sole preserve of the hardened mountain walker – although there are some taxing stages and a few delicate exposed sections that might give an understandable twinge of concern to first-time wanderers among the Alps. Most days lead into a touch of 'civilisation', albeit sometimes this civilisation might be just a small

Refuge de la Gentiane la Barma in Val des Dix (Stage 7)

mountain village with few amenities. Every night there will be a lodging place with the possibility of meals provided, thereby making it unnecessary to carry camping or cooking equipment. Backpacking on this route is a choice, not an obligation.

Lodgings on the Walker's Haute Route are in themselves very much a part of the mountain experience. In villages they allow you to capture some of the region's culture. In remote mountain huts the wanderer is introduced to the climber's world, with an opportunity to witness high alpine scenes that are normally privy only to the mountaineer.

Accommodation varies from hotels (there are luxuriously appointed hotels in certain villages on the route for those inclined and financially able to make use of them), to gîtes and basic refuges, and mattresses spread on the floor of communal dormitories in the attic of a pension or inn. But those planning to camp must understand that organised campsites are not to be found in all valleys, and that wild camping is officially discouraged in Switzerland.

Wherever lodgings (and campsites) are to be found along the route mention is made in the text. Similarly, wherever alternative methods of transport occur (train, bus, cable-car, etc), brief details are given. This is to aid any walkers who might fall behind their schedule due to bad weather, unseasonal conditions, sickness or just plain weariness.

The walk outlined in this guide may be achieved within a two-week holiday, while those with plenty of time available are given options which would extend the route and increase the overall experience. These options are outlined below. The longest stage demands 7½ hours of walking, but there are several days of only 4 hours each. Some of the less demanding days could be amalgamated by fit trekkers in order to reduce the time required to complete the route, should they not have a full fortnight at their disposal, but it would be a pity to do so. This is a route that deserves to be wandered at a gentle pace; the very best of mountain holidays.

The first stage (Chamonix to Argentière – 2hrs) may be seen as a prelude. Should you arrive late in the day in Chamonix as you would, for example, if you flew from the UK to Geneva and travelled from there by train, then you would probably only have sufficient time to reach Argentière on foot that day. However, if your travel arrangements get you to Chamonix at a reasonable time in the morning (on the overnight train from Paris, for example), it might be feasible to walk all the way to Trient, thus combining two stages for a 7½–8hr day, thereby cutting a day off the overall route allocation.

Stage 12A (St Niklaus to Gasenried) links the original Haute Route with the new finish along the Europaweg, and takes about 1½hrs walking time. However, it is not really

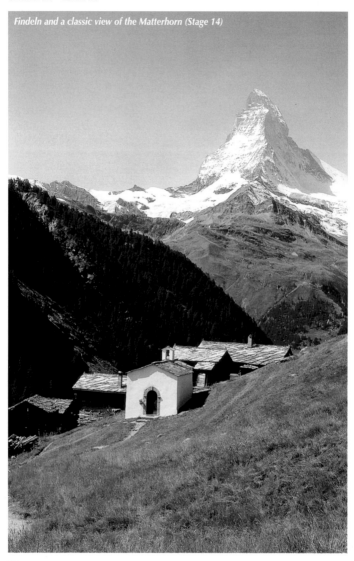

Findeln and a classic view of the Matterhorn (Stage 14)

The Complete Route: 14/15 days	
1	Chamonix – Argentière
2	Argentière – Trient
3	Trient – Champex
4	Champex – Le Châble
5	Le Châble – Cab. Mont Fort
6	Mont Fort – Cab. Prafleuri
7	Prafleuri – Arolla
8	Arolla – La Sage
9	La Sage – Cab. de Moiry
10	Moiry – Zinal
11	Zinal – Gruben
12	Gruben – St Niklaus
12A	St Niklaus – Gasenried (1½hrs walk – or bus)
13	Gasenried – Europa Hut
14	Europa Hut – Zermatt

A 12-day Trek	
1	Chamonix – Trient
2	Trient – Champex
3	Champex – Le Châble
4	Le Châble – Cab. Mont Fort
5	Mont Fort – Cab. Prafleuri
6	Prafleuri – Arolla
7	Arolla – La Sage
8	La Sage – Cab. de Moiry
9	Moiry – Zinal
10	Zinal – Gruben
11	Gruben – St Niklaus
12	St Niklaus – Zermatt

practical to add this short stage to the demanding Augstbordpass crossing (Stage 12), nor to tack it on at the start of Stage 13. If you cannot allow a full day for this walk, it is possible to take a bus from St Niklaus to Gasenried itself – either at the end of Stage 12, or first thing on the morning of Stage 13.

One or two commercial trekking companies follow a large portion of the Walker's Haute Route, but opt for public transport over some sections in order to allow a day or two in Zermatt at the end of a two-week holiday. This is an option available to the individual trekker too, of course. But again, it would be a shame to miss any single stage of this route, for each bears witness to the last and forms a unique link with the next.

GETTING THERE AND BACK AGAIN

Air travel to Switzerland is relatively inexpensive. Regular scheduled flights from the UK are operated principally by British Airways (www.britishairways.com), EasyJet (www.easyjet.com) and Swiss International Airlines (www.swiss.com). Aer Lingus (www.aerlingus.ie) flies from Dublin.

Geneva is the most convenient airport for reaching Chamonix. British Airways currently flies there from London Heathrow and Gatwick,

Birmingham and Manchester. Low-cost EasyJet has regular services from Gatwick, Luton, East Midlands and Liverpool, while Swiss International Airlines operates out of London (Heathrow and City), Birmingham, Manchester and Edinburgh. Aer Lingus has an infrequent service from Dublin.

On arrival at Geneva **onward travel to Chamonix** is either by twice-daily bus from the airport by the French operated SAT Autocar (Tel 04 50 53 01 15), by minibus (www. mountaindropoffs.com, www.cham-van.com), or by train from the airport to Martigny, where you change to the Mont Blanc Express (change again at Le Châtelard on the Swiss/French border).

Travel by rail is straightforward. A superfast London–Paris service is operated by Eurostar through the Channel Tunnel, with onward journey to Chamonix. For up-to-date rail information contact Rail Europe (www.raileurope.com) or European Rail Ltd (www.europeanrail.com)

A low-price alternative worth considering is by **Eurolines overnight coach** from London (Victoria Coach Station) to Chamonix. Bookings can be made through National Express agents or via the Internet (www.eurolines. co.uk). Cut-price promotional fares are often available when booked at least 14 days in advance – conditions include return within a month and no open-dated returns.

Return from Zermatt at the end of the walk will be by train via Visp to Geneva (for flight), to Lausanne (connections for Paris-bound trains) or to Martigny for the Mont Blanc Express route to Chamonix in order to connect with Eurolines return coach to London.

If you don't have reservations from Geneva and are returning by plane, there are probably more and better connections from Zurich airport (reached by train in 3 to 4 hours).

ACCOMMODATION

Practically every village along the route of this walk has a wide selection of accommodation and facilities to choose from, while between villages there are often mountain inns of one sort or another where an overnight lodging may be found. In the early stages there are also several *gîtes d'étape* which are very much like privately owned youth hostels, with (usually) low-cost dormitory accommodation and communal washrooms. In addition there are privately owned mountain huts and others belonging to the Swiss Alpine Club in which non-members can spend a night too.

Outline details are given throughout the text wherever lodgings exist. Telephone numbers are also provided where possible to enable walkers to call ahead to reserve beds – this is especially important during the high season.

It might also be worth noting that the cost of accommodation in Switzerland need not be as prohibitively high as some might fear. Whilst

Hotel Weisshorn, built in 1882 more than 1000m above the valley (Alternative Stage 11)

it is pointless quoting specific prices in a guidebook that could be in print for several years, comparisons with UK costs are very favourable. Bed and breakfast rates in modest hotels used on this route will be on a par with charges made in British establishments, or even cheaper in many cases. And a good and filling evening meal in a Swiss restaurant need cost no more than a pub meal in the UK. Half-pension (*demi-pension/halb-pension*) usually provides the most economical deal. Hotel standards are high, and service will be friendly.

In a few villages along the way it may be possible to rent a private room in a furnished chalet for a night. Some of these rooms have self-catering facilities, otherwise you will need to find a restaurant for your meals. A self-contained room can be economically viable, and where such places are known from personal experience, mention is made in the text. Otherwise, enquire at the local tourist office.

Dortoirs (***matratzenlager*** or *massenlager* in German) are recommended for walkers who do not object to a lack of privacy. Some hotels offer dortoir accommodation in an attic or an outbuilding, while a few establishments are specifically set up as privately run youth hostels – the *gîtes d'étape* mentioned above. In my experience these places offer good value for money. They vary in style, but all provide mixed dormitory accommodation and simple washing facilities. Most have hot showers.

25

Some have individual two-tier bunk beds, others merely offer mattresses on the floor of a large room under the roof. One or two also provide the means for self-catering, whilst the majority offer a full meals service. Those with experience of staying in youth hostels should be more than content with the dortoirs on the Chamonix to Zermatt route.

Mountain huts of the Swiss Alpine Club (SAC) are also used on this route – as well as some that are privately owned. Membership of an affiliated alpine club with reciprocal rights will give reduced overnight fees in SAC huts. (If you are a member of the UK section of the Austrian Alpine Club, for example, do not forget to take your membership card with you.) Members of the British Mountaineering Council (BMC) can also obtain a reciprocal rights card that is recognised here. (Addresses and contact numbers of both the Austrian Alpine Club and BMC will be found in Appendix C.)

Mountain huts have mixed dormitory accommodation. Most of those visited on this route provide meals and drinks (neither Refuge Les Grands on Alternative Stage 2, nor Refuge de la Gentiane la Barma passed on Stage 7, is permanently manned in summer). Evening meals in huts are invariably filling and high in calorific value, but washroom facilities are sometimes rather basic, although a shower is nearly always available.

As for camping, officially approved sites are to be found in a

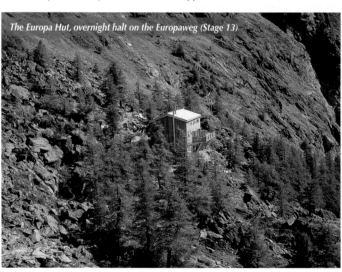

The Europa Hut, overnight halt on the Europaweg (Stage 13)

On arrival at a mountain hut remove your boots before entering and help yourself to a pair of hut shoes found on a rack just inside the door. Locate the guardian to book bedspace for the night and put your name down for any meals you may require. There will sometimes be a choice of menu, but not always. Blankets and pillows are provided in the dormitories, but a sleeping bag liner is well worth carrying with you for purposes of hygiene. Some of these huts are used by climbers who may need to make a pre-dawn start, and whilst your sleep may be disturbed by those leaving early, it is important that you do not disturb others if you go to bed after they have settled. Lights out is normally 10pm, if you last that long!

number of valleys along the route, but certainly not in all of them. Where they do exist facilities range from adequate to good. Off-site camping is officially discouraged in Switzerland since grasslands form a valuable part of the agricultural economy, and although it would not be beyond the bounds of possibility for individual backpackers to find a discreet corner of an alp for a single night's stay, it would be irresponsible to indicate likely sites in this book. Wherever possible please ask permission of farmers. It has always been my experience in Switzerland that whenever a farmer has been approached, permission has readily been granted and a good site pointed out. In all cases, wherever you camp be discreet, take care not to foul water supplies, light no fires and pack all litter away with you.

Mention of any establishment in this book, whether as an overnight lodging or as a place where refreshments may be had, should not

necessarily be taken as an endorsement of services on offer.

WHEN TO GO

The best time to tackle any high-level trek in the Alps will be dictated by the amount and timing of the previous winter's snowfall and the onset of cold, inclement weather in the autumn. As the Walker's Haute Route crosses several high passes and negotiates some remote and difficult terrain where a lot of snow cover could create problems or even danger, it is not advisable in a 'normal' year to consider setting out before early July. During some years even that could be too soon, although one would normally expect most of the snow (and with it the risk of avalanche) to have gone by then, and flowers to be in full bloom. But do bear in mind that it is not unusual for parts of the Alps to have a sudden dump of snow even in the middle of August.

The only certainty when it comes to predicting alpine weather is that any long-distance forecast is bound to be unpredictable!

In the high summer period of July to the middle of August, when the trails are at their busiest, temperatures can rise to 25–30°C even at altitudes of 2500m and more, and frequent thunderstorms may be expected, usually from mid-afternoon on.

Autumn begins in mid-September, often bringing long periods of fine weather with clear skies by day and the first frosts at night. By the end of September a number of huts will close, except for a simple 'winter room' which remains open with basic amenities. October can be magical when the larchwoods turn to gold and shrubs on the hillsides are ablaze with scarlet leaves. But heavy rain, and the first of winter's snow falling on the higher hills, can restrict high-altitude walking, or at least reduce its pleasure.

Perhaps the most favourable period to trek the Walker's Haute Route, from both a weather perspective and also for availability of accommodation, is from mid-August to the middle of September.

Day-to-day weather forecasts, in German, French or Italian, may be obtained in Switzerland by telephone (Tel 162), while daily and five-day forecasts are available on www.meteoschweiz.ch/en. Local tourist information offices and guides' bureaux often display a 2–3 day forecast, and sometimes there's a barometer on show by which you can check pressure trends. Up-to-date advice may also be sought from the guardians at mountain huts.

Le Châble is approached through meadows in the Val de Bagnes (Stage 4)

Those who tackle the Chamonix to Zermatt route will reap countless rewards. And those rewards will be more easily gathered if you are physically fit and mentally attuned. Crossing the grain of the country means that there will be many steep uphill and downhill sections to face, and since it is important to enjoy every aspect of the first pass as much as the last, fitness should be there from the very beginning.

Taking regular exercise at home will go some way towards getting in condition for the physical demands of the route. Of course, the best way to prepare yourself for a mountain walking holiday is by walking. Uphill. Carry a rucksack with a few belongings in it to accustom your shoulders to the weight. If on the first day out from Chamonix your lungs and legs complain, then you've probably not done enough to get fit, and the crossing of Col de Balme will be less enjoyable than it deserves.

Mental fitness is as important as the physical, and the two often go hand in hand. If you gaze with dread at the amount of height to be gained in order to cross a pass, no doubt you will suffer in consequence. Let every day be greeted with eagerness. Find joy in the steep uphill as well as the downward slope. Draw strength from the beauty of the scenes around you. Enjoy the movement of clouds, the wind and wildness as much as the gleam of sunshine; the raw crags and

screes of desolation as well as the lush flower-strewn pastures and distant snowscapes. Each is an integral part of the mountain world; a world of magic and mystery. It's a world through which it is a privilege to move in freedom. Don't take a moment of this experience for granted.

Since walking across mountains is thirsty work, you'll need to start each day with a full water bottle – at least 1 litre per person. And there's a good chance that you'll need to top up during the day too. On a number of stages there will be a water trough fed by a spring located near farm buildings or in a pasture. Filling your bottle from the feeder pipe should be perfectly safe. As for taking water directly from streams, in more than 40 years of trekking in the Alps, I've never had any problems from drinking from mountain streams as long as they're fast running and located above any grazing animals. But to be safe, it would be advisable to treat stream water with purification tablets, available from pharmacies or specialist outdoor retailers.

As for clothing and equipment, what you choose to take will be crucial to your overall enjoyment of the trek.
- Boots need to be lightweight, comfortable, fit well and be broken in before leaving home. They should give ankle support and have thick cleated soles (Vibram or similar) with plenty of grip.

- Good waterproofs are essential, not just as protection from rain or snowfall, but to double as wind-proofs. Jacket and overtrousers made from a 'breathable' material are recommended. Bearing in mind that some of the passes are almost 3000m high, a warm pullover or pile jacket should also be taken, as should a woollen hat or balaclava, and gloves. A lightweight collapsible umbrella can be indispensable for those who wear glasses.

- It is also necessary to take preventative action against long periods of extreme heat and unshaded sun. A brimmed sunhat, suncream (factor 25 or stronger) and sunglasses should be part of your equipment.

- A first-aid kit must be included (see under 'Safety in the Mountains'). Waterbottle, compass, headtorch and spare batteries, whistle and maps should also be carried, as should a small amount of emergency food. (This can be recharged regularly as you pass through villages.)

- A sheet sleeping bag (sleeping bag liner) is highly recommended for use in dortoirs and mountain huts. A conventional sleeping bag, however, will not be needed unless you plan to camp.

- A lightweight towel and personal toiletry items (plus toilet paper and lighter).

- Telescopic trekking poles will ease the strain on legs and knees, especially on the many steep downhill sections.

- Bivvy bag (or space blanket) in case of emergencies.

- A comfortable rucksack with waist-belt adjusted to take the weight of your pack is important. You should be able to keep equipment down to 10kg (20lb) at most – unless you plan to backpack with full camping gear, that is. A waterproof cover is essential, plus stuffsacs or a large thick polythene bag so you can pack all your equipment inside the sack. Doing so should protect items from getting damp in the event of bad weather. A selection of plastic bags of assorted sizes will also be useful.

- If travelling in June (or even early July) ice axe and crampons may be necessary. Call huts or tourist offices to check.

LANGUAGES

On all but the final two valleys of the walk the route passes through French-speaking territory, but once you cross from Zinal into the Turtmanntal German becomes the official language. Although the non-linguist may have difficulty conversing in general terms with locals met in the mountains, English is widely understood in most of the villages, and you will probably face no real language problems in hotels or other lodgings. The Appendix contains a glossary of French and German words likely to be met along the way, but is no substitute for either a pocket dictionary or a phrase-book.

PATHS AND WAYMARKS

Most of the paths adopted by this route will have been in use for centuries by farmers, traders and hunters going about their daily business – from alp to alp, or from one valley to the next by way of an ancient pass. A few will be of recent origin, either laid out by a local commune, by a branch of the Swiss Footpath Protection Association, by the Valais Rambling Association (Association Valaisanne de la Randonnée Pédestre) or by members of the SAC in order to reach a mountain hut.

There are two official types of footpath in Switzerland which are signposted and waymarked to a common standard. A *chemin pedestre* (*wanderweg*) is a path that remains either in the valley or along the hillsides at a modest altitude. These are maintained and graded at a more gentle angle than the *chemin de montagne* or *bergweg*. Yellow metal signposts bear the names of major landmark destinations such as a pass, lake, hut or village, often with estimated times given in hours (*Heures* in French, *Stunden* in German-speaking regions) and minutes (*Min*). A white plate on these yellow signs names the immediate locality and, sometimes, the altitude. Along the trail occasional yellow signs or paint flashes on rocks are also found.

A mountain path (*chemin de montagne* or *bergweg*) is one which ventures higher and is more demanding than the *chemin pedestre/wanderweg*. These paths will usually be rougher,

Trail markers at the path junction above the Pas du Chat (Stage 7)

narrower and sometimes fading if not in regular use. Signposting will be similar to that already described, except that the outer sections of the finger post will be painted red and white, and the intermediate paint flashes along the way will be blazed white–red–white. Occasional cairns may also be used to direct the way over boulder slopes, or where poor visibility could create difficulties. In the event of mist or low cloud obscuring the onward route, it is essential to study the area of visibility with the utmost care before venturing on to the next paint flash or stone-built cairn. In extreme cases it may be necessary to take compass bearings and make progress from one to the other in this manner.

A third type of waymarking may also be encountered. This is the blue and white stripe of an *Alpine Route* that signifies a more challenging route which may involve glacier crossing or some scrambling.

Currently the most difficult paths are found on:

1 Stage 3 on the descent from the Fenêtre d'Arpette to Champex;
2 Stage 6 between Col de Louvie and Col de Prafleuri where the route makes a traverse of a large area of rocks and boulders;
3 on the approach to Col de la Chaux on Alternative Stage 6;
4 on the approach to, and crossing of, Col de Riedmatten (Stage 7); and
5 along the Europaweg on the final two stages leading to Zermatt.

On this impressive and visually spectacular trail many exposed sections have been safeguarded with fixed rope handrails, and on several occasions the way crosses potentially hazardous areas where rockfall is a concern. Warning signs have been fixed that urge walkers to hurry across the danger areas.

SAFETY IN THE MOUNTAINS

Whilst the route is mostly well signed (without ever mentioning the Chamonix to Zermatt Haute Route) with good paths for the majority of the way, and there are working farms and villages at frequent intervals along the route, there are also wild and remote sections where an accident could have serious consequences. It should be recognised that participation in any mountain activity places a need for personal responsibility and self-reliance, for all mountain areas – the Alps as much as any – contain a variety of objective dangers for the unwary, and the long-distance walker should be prepared to deal with any hazards that arise.

Plan each day's walk carefully. Study the route outline, the amount of height to be gained and lost, and the time required to reach your destination. None of the stages described are particularly long, but in case you are tempted to double up, make sure you have enough hours of daylight in which to cross the day's pass and descend to the safety of the next valley, or to where a night's lodging may be had, before nightfall. Carry a few emergency food rations and a first-aid kit. (It would be sensible to invest in good first-aid training – not just for the C–Z trek, but for everyday emergencies.) Know how to read a map and compass, and watch for signs of deteriorating weather. Never be too proud to turn back if it is safer to do so than to continue in the face of an on-coming storm or on a trail that has become unjustifiably dangerous.

In the unhappy event of an accident, stay calm. Move yourself and, if feasible, the injured person (with care not to aggravate the injury) away from any imminent danger of stonefall or avalanche, and apply immediate first aid. Keep the victim warm, using any spare clothes available. Make a careful written note of the precise location and assessment of the injury, and if you have a mobile phone (and can get a signal) call for assistance: Tel 144, or Tel 1414 which calls out helicopter rescue – this should only be used if absolutely essential. Alternatively, send for help whilst someone remains with the injured member.

The international distress call is a series of six signals (blasts on a whistle and – after dark – flashes with a torch) spaced evenly for a minute, followed by one minute's pause, then repeat with a further six signals. The reply is three signals per minute followed by a minute's pause.

There is **no free mountain rescue service** in Switzerland and no free hospital treatment but EHIC cards for European and Australian visitors are valid. The result of an emergency could therefore be extremely costly. Be adequately insured, and be cautious. The addresses of several specialist insurance companies dealing with mountain walking/trekking holidays are given in Appendix C.

Leave a copy of your travel itinerary and insurance details with a

THE FIRST AID KIT

All walkers should carry a basic first-aid kit comprising:

- antihistamine cream
- antispetic cream
- antiseptic wipes
- aspirin
- blister kit (Compeed)
- crêpe bandage
- finger bandage
- immodium capsules (in case of diarrhoea)
- latex gloves
- painkillers
- plasters
- safety pins
- scissors
- triangular bandage
- tweezers
- water purification tablets
- wound dressing

responsible friend or relative at home, and to carry with you photocopies of important documents – information pages of your passport, insurance certificate, travel tickets, etc – as well as an emergency home contact address and telephone number.

FLORA AND FAUNA

The Pennine Alps contain the richest flora in all Switzerland. One of the factors responsible for this is the mixture of limestone, gneiss and schistose rocks, which encourages calcipile (lime-loving) plants to flourish in some areas, and calcifuge varieties in others. Climatic considerations also play an important role, as does the marked difference in altitude between valley bed and the upper plant zone. Walkers who daily cross the high passes in a traverse of the region – particularly in the early summer – will wander through a number of successive plant zones, and it's not necessary to be a trained botanist to enjoy the variety of flowers and shrubs on show. There are, however, several handy well-illustrated guidebooks available that provide at-a-glance information on specific flowers such as *Alpine Flowers* by Gillian Price (Cicerone 2014).

There will be all the expected varieties, from gentian to edelweiss, from alpenrose to crimson-eyed primulas, and many more besides. This is not the place to list them all. Newcomers to the Alps may be surprised to find that it is not only the meadowlands that reward with bloom, but that even the high,

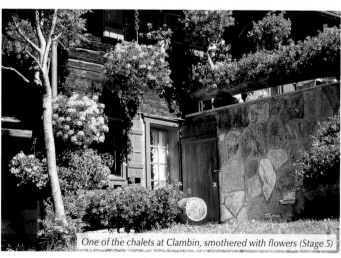

One of the chalets at Clambin, smothered with flowers (Stage 5)

seemingly lifeless cliff faces, screes and glacier-bordering moraines have their own species of flowering plants, and it is often such discoveries that make days in the mountains so memorable.

Of all creatures native to the Alps the one most likely to be seen on this walk is the engaging marmot (*Marmota marmota*). On many days you will no doubt first hear a sharp shrill whistle as you cross a boulder slope or wander a high alp on the borders of grassland and scree. This is the marmot's warning cry, and you may then see two or three brown furry creatures scurrying for cover.

The marmot is a gregarious animal, living in colonies among a variety of mountain and valley locations in burrows whose entrance holes may be seen from some of the footpaths on the walk. They grow to the size of a large hare and weigh up to 10kg (22lb), hibernating in winter for around five months, then emerging in spring when the snow cover melts. Their young are born during the early summer when you may be lucky enough to catch sight of kitten-sized creatures romping or playfully fighting in the short grass of the upper hillsides.

Chamois (*Rupicapra rupicapra*), or *Gemse* in German, are rarely seen at close quarters, but in the high mountain regions just below the snowline, it is not unusual to spy a small herd picking its way with commendable ease over excessively steep terrain. On occasion they can be seen grazing on the forest fringe. From a distance it is possible to mistake chamois, with their small curving horns, for female or young ibex. Ibex, however, have a stockier body.

Ibex (*Capra ibex*) are also known as *bouquetin* (French) or *steinbock* (German). These squat, sturdy animals live and graze in herds – one noble buck with a harem of females. The male sports a pair of majestic, scimitar-shaped horns marked with a series of knobbles, like arthritic joints, that are used in battle as they fight for control over the herds, usually in the autumn rut.

On the scenic belvedere from Cabane du Mont Fort to Col Termin, known as the *Sentier des Chamois* (Stage 6), ibex are likely to be seen at close quarters. A large herd lives nearby on a hillside designated as a wildlife sanctuary. Another herd may be seen near Cabane de Prafleuri.

RECOMMENDED MAPS

Maps of the Swiss survey, Landeskarte der Schweiz (LS/Carte nationale de la Suisse, www.swiss topo.ch/en), are among the finest in the world. By artistic use of shading, contours and colouring, the line of ridges and rock faces, the flow of glaciers and streams, the curve of an amphitheatre, narrow cut of a glen, the expanse of a lake and forest cover of a hillside all announce themselves clearly. A picture of the country immediately leaps from the paper.

At the head of each stage of the walk a note is given with regard to the specific map recommended for that particular stretch. In each case I have chosen the 1:50,000 series as this should be perfectly adequate for most needs. The greater detail provided by the 1:25,000 series is not likely to be required on this route, given the amount of waymarking on the ground. (No less than nine sheets would be needed of 1:25,000 scale.)

Standard coverage at 1:50,000 scale runs into five sheets (numbers 282T, 283T, 273T, 274T and 284T), each of which highlights major walking routes in red. Though not highlighting individual routes, the LS has

also published two large sheets which cover the whole area crossed by the Walker's Haute Route. These are:

- 5027T Grand St-Bernard, Combins – Arolla
- 5028T Monta Rosa – Matterhorn.

In addition, there is a new series of Kümmerley + Frey 1:60,000 walking maps printed on waterproof paper. The route is covered by sheets:

- 22 Grand St Bernard – Dents du Midi (although barely adequate for the stretch in France)
- 23 Val d'Anniviers/Val d'Hérens
- 24 Zermatt – Sass Fee.

Addresses of map suppliers are given in Appendix C.

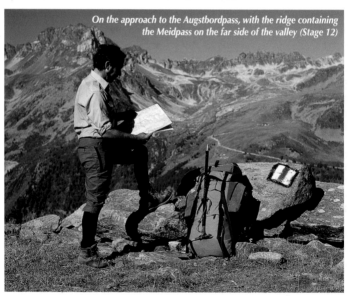

On the approach to the Augstbordpass, with the ridge containing the Meidpass on the far side of the valley (Stage 12)

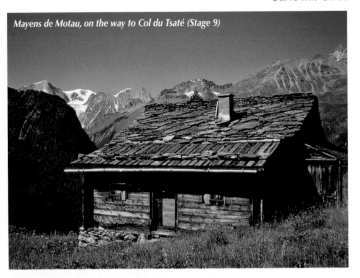

Mayens de Motau, on the way to Col du Tsaté (Stage 9)

USING THIS GUIDE

A brief word of explanation about this guidebook. Distances are given throughout in kilometres and metres. Heights quoted are in metric too. These details are taken directly from the map, but in attempting to measure the actual distance of each day's walk I have made the nearest estimation I could. (With countless zig-zags it is impossible to be precise and some GPS users have pointed out that the distances covered may be slightly longer than indicated.)

Likewise, times are approximate only and make no allowance for rest stops or photographic interruptions – for these you will need to add another 25–50% to the day's total. Inevitably these times will be found slow by some walkers, fast by others. By comparing your times with those given here (or quoted on signposts along the route) you will soon discover how much our pace differs, and adjustments can then be made when calculating your own progress through the day.

Throughout the text route directions 'left' and 'right' apply to the direction of travel, whether in ascent, descent or traverse. However, when used in reference to the banks of glaciers or streams, 'left' and 'right' indicate the direction of flow, ie: looking downwards. Where doubts might occur a compass direction is also given.

I have attempted to avoid an over-use of abbreviations in the guide, but it is inevitable that some have been

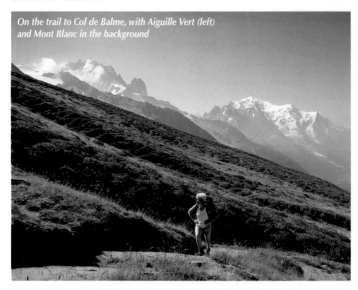

On the trail to Col de Balme, with Aiguille Vert (left) and Mont Blanc in the background

adopted. All should be easily understood, but the following list is given for clarification:

- ATM   cashpoints
- C–Z   Chamonix to Zermatt, the Walker's Haute Route
- hrs   hours
- km   kilometres
- LS   Landeskarte der Schweiz (maps)
- m   metres
- mins   minutes
- PTT   Post Office (Post, Telephone & Telegraph)
- SAC   Swiss Alpine Club
- TGV   Trains à Grande Vitesse (the French superfast train)
- TMB   Tour of Mont Blanc

Finally, I have made every effort to check the route as described for accuracy, and it is to the best of my belief that the guidebook goes to press with all details correct. However, changes do occur from time to time with paths re-routed and certain landmarks altered. Any corrections required to keep the book up to date will be made in future printings where possible. Should you discover any changes that are necessary (or can recommend additions with regard to accommodation, places of refreshment and so on) I would very much appreciate a brief note to that effect. A postcard or email sent to me via the publisher would be gratefully received.

INFORMATION AT A GLANCE

Currencies From Chamonix to Col de Balme (Stages 1–2) the Euro is used; thereafter it's the Swiss franc (CHF) – 100 centimes/rappen = CHF1. But note that the Euro is often acceptable in Trient and Champex, although change will be given in Swiss francs. Most credit cards are acceptable in Swiss hotels, but cash will usually be needed in mountain huts. Carry plenty of ready cash with you as there are few ATMs and even fewer banks along the route.

Formalities Visas are not required in France or Switzerland for holders of a valid UK passport or other EU nationals. Visitors from other countries should enquire at their local French and Swiss embassies.

Health precautions At the time of writing no vaccinations are required by visitors entering France or Switzerland unless they've been in an infected area within 14 days of arrival. Although there are no endemic contageous diseases here, along with much of Central Europe the Ixodes tick (whose bite can cause TBE – tick-borne encephilitis) exists in several alpine regions. Risk is seasonal, from March to September, so summer trekkers may be vulnerable. An injection of TBE immunoglobulin gives short-term protection; ask your GP for advice. Any medical treatment in Switzerland must be paid for, but note that the European Health Insurance Card (EHIC) is valid in both France and Switzerland – but note its limitations. It is no substitute for health insurance, so make sure you have adequate cover that includes personal accident, sickness and rescue. (See Appendix C for a list of specialist insurers.)

International dialling codes When phoning to France from the UK, use 0033; for Switzerland use 0041. To phone the UK from France or Switzerland, the code is 0044. In all cases remember to delete the initial 0 of the area code after dialling the international code. Cashless call boxes operated by phonecard are the norm in both France and Switzerland. Telephone cards (Télécarte in France, Taxcard in Switzerland) may be bought in post offices, tobacconists, newsagents and some railway stations.

Languages spoken French is the main language spoken throughout the Walker's Haute Route until you reach the Turtmanntal on Stage 11/Alternative Stage 11A; thereafter it is German – or rather, Schwyzerdütsch. English is understood in many of the hotels, dortoirs and refuges along the way, but an effort to communicate in the local language will be appreciated.

Weather on the web www.meteofrance.com provides three-day forecasts. For the Swiss Alps try www.meteoschweiz.ch/en which gives daily and five-day forecasts.

STAGE 1
Chamonix – Argentière

Start	Chamonix (1037m)
Distance	9km
Height gain	214m
Time	2hrs
High point	Argentière (1251m)
Map(s)	LS 5027T Grand St Bernard–Combins–Arolla 1:50,000 or LS 282T Martigny 1:50,000
Transport options	Train & bus (Chamonix–Argentière)
Accommodation	Chamonix – hotels, youth hostel, camping
	Les Praz de Chamonix (35mins) – hotels, camping
	Argentière – hotels, gîte

This initial, very short stage is suggested as a prelude for walkers who arrive in Chamonix late in the day and wish to get a few kilometres under their boots before seeking overnight accommodation. Those who arrive early and fresh enough from their travels can, of course, combine this with Stage 2 and continue over Col de Balme to Trient for an eight-hour day.

It's a valley walk without any passes to tackle. But it's a pleasant valley walk all the same, with a few short ascents to contend with. It begins by threading a way among the crowds that throng the streets of Chamonix and heads upvalley on the road leading out of town, but then takes a path through woods and across open glades with a wonderful introductory view of the Drus standing guard over the Mer de Glace. Crossing the Arveyron the walk enters Les Praz de Chamonix, then over the river Arve onto another woodland path that is followed most of the way to Argentière.

Chamonix's valley is dominated by the Mont Blanc massif whose jagged aiguilles form fenceposts of granite and whose glaciers hang in sheets of arctic splendour above the town and its neighbouring forests. On the walk to Argentière there are several opportunities to gaze upon such scenes, while the bare northern wall with the russet-coloured Aiguilles Rouges is largely hidden from view.

As early as 1741 Chamonix – then a small village – was 'discovered' by Richard Pococke and William Windham, whose *Account of the Glaciers or Ice Alps in Savoy* sowed the seeds of popularity for the valley; a popularity that has steadily increased from a lowly trickle to the present-day deluge of tourists who threaten an overkill, with almost a million visitors per year in Chamonix alone.

Footpaths along the valley are busy during the summer, and will remain so for the first three stages; that is, until the route of the Tour of Mont Blanc (TMB) has been left behind. During the high season there's likely to be a heavy demand for accommodation. A phone call in advance is recommended.

CHAMONIX (1037M)

With the close proximity of Mont Blanc, Chamonix has always been at the forefront of alpine mountaineering, and during the development of alpinism in the 19th century it became a serious rival to Zermatt. Today it is unquestionably the leading mountaineering centre of Europe, if not the world. But the town's importance extends beyond the limits of mountaineering, for in winter it is a major ski resort, while in summer it attracts a deluge of general tourists. Chamonix has plenty to occupy them, including the cable-car to the summit of the Aiguille du Midi, and from there the possibility of traversing the whole range by cableway to Entrèves, near Courmayeur in Italy. The railway to Montenvers has long been one of the most popular excursions, with its climax being superb views along the Mer de Glace to the Grandes Jorasses. The Chamonix valley, of course, offers excellent walking opportunities. See *Mont Blanc Walks* by Hilary Sharp (Cicerone Press). Although the classic Tour du Mont Blanc does not actually visit Chamonix itself, it does traverse the valley. See *Tour of Mont Blanc* by Kev Reynolds (Cicerone Press).

Hotels, youth hostel, camping, restaurants, shops, banks, PTT, tourist information, railway, buses, cableways and funicular, **www.chamonix.com**.

From Chamonix railway station walk down the main street, Avenue Michel Croz, alongside shops and restaurants, and take the first road breaking to the right. This is Rue Whymper, which leads to a roundabout opposite the Ecole Nationale de Ski et l'Alpinisme. Continue straight ahead along the road signed to Les Praz and Argentière, soon leaving the town behind.

Shortly after passing the Chamonix–Mont Blanc road sign (15mins from the station) note a bus stop on the left, and a sign on the right to La Frasse and Les Coverays. Immediately after the bus stop turn left over

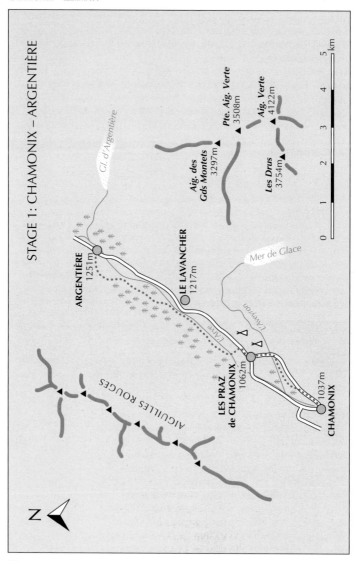

STAGE 1: CHAMONIX – ARGENTIÈRE

a bridge, then take the right-hand of two paths. This leads through the Bois du Bouchet. On coming to a crossing track turn right and soon gain a very fine view of the spear-like Drus ahead. At a crossing road continue ahead, and when the path veers right to enter a tunnel, leave it in favour of a minor path which takes you onto the road where it crosses the Arveyron (30 mins). Turn left and walk into

LES PRAZ DE CHAMONIX
(1062m, 35mins, hotels, camping, restaurants)

When you reach a roundabout cross directly ahead beside a small church in the direction of Argentière and Martigny. Immediately after passing the Hotel Les Rhododendrons the road curves to the right where you gain another splendid view of the Drus. Take the first turning left and wander past the Hotel Le Labrador. Through a

The Aiguille du Drus, seen from Les Praz de Chamonix on the way to Argentière

43

golf club car park continue ahead on a gravel track which soon crosses the river Arve. Ignore the initial path on the right, but stay on the track which curves right just beyond. The track becomes a narrow metalled lane. When it forks continue ahead and shortly come to the café/bar Le Paradis des Praz (refreshments). Beyond this the way continues as a pleasant forest walk beside a stream.

Ignore all bridges that tempt across to the right-hand side of the Arve, and at path junctions follow signs for Argentière. About 1hr 5mins from the start the way forks near the Pont de la Corva (1092m). Do not cross the bridge, but stay on the left of the river and climb the wooded slope on the Petit Balcon Sud. From here to Argentière there are several junctions, all well signed. Remain on the Petit Balcon Sud; in woods most of the way it's an undulating trail which climbs to a maximum altitude of about 1230m, then slopes downhill only to climb again. There are numerous bench seats, but few open views.

The path takes you down almost to the level of the railway, follows it for a short distance then climbs briefly before sloping downhill again, coming onto a track by some houses. Walk ahead along the track to arrive in the main street in

ARGENTIÈRE (1251M)

A compact village at the upper end of the Chamonix valley. The original village stands on the true left bank of the Arve below the terminal moraine of the Argentière Glacier, an attractive huddle of chalets and a small church. Argentière makes a low-key alternative to Chamonix for a mountaineering or skiing base. The 'new' village which has grown astride the main valley road has a range of accommodation, plenty of restaurants, food stores and a tourist information office.

Accommodation: Gîte d'étape Le Belvedere, 52 dortoir places, meals provided (Tel 04 50 18 50 66); lower priced hotel: Hotel des Randonneurs (Tel 04 50 54 02 80). Restaurants, shops, PTT, tourist information (Tel 04 50 54 02 14), railway and bus links with Chamonix.

If you have difficulty finding accommodation in Argentière, try Gîte d'étape Les Moulin in Les Frasserands (38 places, open all year; Tel 04 50 54 05 37 and 06 82 33 34 54), about 2km upvalley.

THE GOLDEN AGE OF MOUNTAINEERING

The Haute Route begins by wandering down **Avenue Michel Croz**, named after one of the finest guides of the Golden Age of Mountaineering, a man whose talent and skills were discovered by Alfred Wills and then put to good use by Edward Whymper. Croz was a Chamonix guide (born in Le Tour in 1830) whose list of first ascents includes the Barre des Écrins, Mont Dolent, Aiguille d'Argentière, Dent Blanche, Grandes Jorasses and the crossing of the Moming Pass above Zinal. In 1865 Croz was in Whymper's party that made the first ascent of the Matterhorn, but was tragically killed on the descent. (See *Scrambles Amongst the Alps* by Edward Whymper.)

On leaving Avenue Michel Croz the route turns into Rue Whymper. **Edward Whymper** will forever be remembered as the man who first climbed the Matterhorn, and as such is known far beyond the somewhat limited circle of active mountaineers. Whymper was a London-born wood engraver who first visited the Alps in 1860 in order to make a series of sketches for the publisher William Longman. The following year he began a remarkable climbing career (often with Michel Croz) that included first ascents of the Barre des Écrins, the aiguilles of Trélatête and Argentière, Grand Cornier, Grandes Jorasses (west summit), Aiguille Verte and, of course, the Matterhorn.

He did little climbing in the Alps after the Matterhorn tragedy, but explored farther afield – making journeys to Greenland, the Andes of South America and three trips to the Canadian Rockies. His *Scrambles Amongst the Alps* is still considered to be one of the finest of all mountaineering books, and is frequently republished. Whymper died in Chamonix at the age of 71.

STAGE 2

Argentière – Col de Balme – Trient

Start	Argentière (1251m)
Distance	12km
Height gain	953m
Height loss	925m
Time	5–5½hrs
High point	Col de Balme (2204m)
Map(s)	LS 5027T Grand St Bernard–Combins–Arolla 1:50,000 or LS 282T Martigny 1:50,000
Transport options	Bus (Argentière–Le Tour) Gondola and chairlift (Le Tour–Charamillon–Les Grandes Otanes near Col de Balme)
Accommodation	Le Tour (1hr 30mins) – hotel, gîte Col de Balme (3hrs) – refuge Le Peuty (5hrs 15mins) – gîte, camping Trient – dortoirs
Alternative route	Col de Balme to Trient via L'Arolette

For a first full day's walking this is a convenient and relatively undemanding stage. There's plenty of height to gain and lose, but the crossing of Col de Balme is not at all severe and walkers fresh from the UK have an opportunity to get into their stride with ease. Views on the way to the pass, when you look back through the length of the Chamonix valley, are dominated by Mont Blanc and its aiguilles, while the col itself gives a magnificent vision of the Monarch of the Alps shining its great snow dome and sending long glacial tentacles into the valley.

The Swiss frontier runs through Col de Balme, so all the descent (and the rest of the walk to Zermatt) will be within Swiss territory. Vistas of Mont Blanc are shunted into memory, although in days to come sudden surprise views will draw the eye back to the west and that great crown of snow.

The valley of Trient into which you descend is green and pastoral. There are no major peaks nearby, of either snow or rock, to match the grandeur of France behind you, but the scene from the col is not short of beauty, for to the north a line of mountains indicates the crest of the Bernese Alps, with Les Diablerets, Wildhorn and Wildstrubel just discernible.

From the centre of Argentière take the road to the right (east), to pass the village post office and Office du Tourisme, and cross the river (l'Arve) with the Glacier d'Argentière seen directly ahead.

> The **Glacier d'Argentière** flows from the great basin formed by the curving ridges of the Tour Noir, Mont Dolent, Aiguille de Triolet, Les Courtes and Les Droites. Mont Dolent is the lynchpin of this system, and on its summit the frontiers of France, Italy and Switzerland meet.

At a junction of streets bear right into the Chemin de la Moraine, and you will come to the line of the Mont Blanc Express railway. Pass beneath this and onto a track going ahead towards woods where you join the Petit Balcon Nord. Shortly after passing a chalet on the right, you'll see another set back on the left. On coming to a second chalet on the left, take the path beside it which joins the main Petit Balcon Nord at a signed junction. Turn left towards Le Tour.

Rising steadily among trees you will come to a path junction (20mins) where you continue straight ahead. In another 20mins there's a second junction where again you keep ahead. Emerging from the woods the path

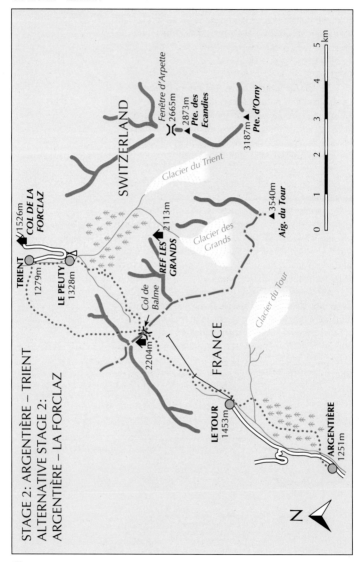

STAGE 2: ARGENTIÈRE – TRIENT
ALTERNATIVE STAGE 2:
ARGENTIÈRE – LA FORCLAZ

narrows and gradually loses height with the village of Le Tour seen below. Cross a stream draining the Glacier du Tour and walk on into

LE TOUR (1453m, 1–1½hrs) Accommodation: Chalet Alpin du Tour [CAF gîte] 87 places, open April to end of September (Tel 04 50 54 04 16, **www.clubalpin-chamonix.com**); Hotel l'Olympique (Tel 04 50 54 01 04). Restaurant, water supply, public toilets, telephone, bus to Chamonix, gondola lift to Charamillon.

Walk to the roadhead by the Télécabin Le Tour Col de Balme. ▶

The main path to Col de Balme passes along the right-hand side of the gondola lift station, and continues ahead on a broad track/ski piste. About 10mins from the gondola station a signed path strikes ahead to the right and twists up to the middle station of the gondola lift (**CHARAMILLON** 1850m, refreshments).

Above Charamillon a path branches to the right away from the main track on the way to the popular Albert Premier refuge, first passing the **Gîte d'Alpage** (20 places, open mid-June to mid-September (Tel 04 50 54 17 07), refreshments). Ignore this option and maintain direction; when the track forks by a ski tow continue ahead, but 2mins later take a steep path which rises above the track. The gradient soon eases and the path gains height without undue effort to reach the

CHALET-REFUGE COL DE BALME (2204m, 3–3½hrs) The refuge has 26 places, open end of June to mid-September (Tel 04 50 54 02 33). It stands on the unmarked Franco/Swiss border and purchases can be made in either Euros or Swiss francs.

Standing astride the Franco/Swiss border on the Col de Balme with a magnificent view of the Mont Blanc range ('If that view does not thrill you you are better away from the Alps,' wrote RLG Irving),

If you prefer to take the easy way to Col de Balme, ride the gondola lift to Charamillon, then take the chairlift to Les Grandes Otanes, from which a short contouring path leads to the col.

the **Chalet-Refuge Col de Balme** – or rather its predecessors – was for centuries a bone of contention between the men of Chamonix and those of Swiss Valais, and was burnt down and rebuilt several times. It's interesting to note that the col is measured at 2191m by the French, and 2204m by the Swiss. As the refuge is entered from the Swiss side, it's reckoned to be in Swiss territory, although its telephone number is French.

Looking back from the Col de Balme path, Mont Blanc dominates, while Le Tour nestles below

The col makes a wonderful viewpoint. To the south stands the snowy mass of Mont Blanc and its guardian aiguilles – Aiguille Verte and Drus being predominant in that view, while the Aiguilles Rouges line the right-hand wall of the valley.

Mont Blanc on the left, with the Aiguilles Rouges on the right, seen from the path to Col de Balme

MONT BLANC

As the highest mountain in Western Europe Mont Blanc (4807m) has been the focus of mountaineering attention for more than two centuries. In 1760 wealthy Geneva scientist Horace-Bénédict de Saussure (1740–99) offered a prize for the first man to reach its summit. Several attempts were made in the ensuing years, but it was not until 8 August 1786 that Michel-Gabriel Páccard, the Chamonix doctor, and Jacques Balmat, a crystal hunter, reached the top. (Saussure himself made the third ascent in 1787.) Tourist ascents followed, then attention was focused on neighbouring aiguilles and new routes to already claimed summits.

Among the outstanding developments mention should be made of the Brenva Ridge in 1865, Peuterey Ridge (1927), Route Major (1928), Gervasutti Pillar (1951) and Central Pillar of Freney in 1961. But whilst practically every face, pillar, ridge and couloir has been explored, Mont Blanc still retains its charisma, and to non-mountaineers no less, its undisputed grace and beauty. (For a history of the mountain, see *Savage Snows* by Walt Unsworth (Hodder & Stoughton, 1986).)

Groups of ebullient walkers occupied all the seats outside the refuge, and most of those inside too. To a man (and a woman) they were all tackling the TMB and enjoying the cameraderie such a sociable walk inspires, greeting each new arrival with rude remarks, having established an easy rapport during the days in which they'd shared the same paths, valleys and passes. They were heading south on the closing stages of their classic walk, while we were going in the opposite direction, against the tide, as it were. I looked back at Mont Blanc, then ahead to a grid of distant ridges that both teased and enticed. Col de Balme held the key to a wonderland.

There are three ways in which to continue from Col de Balme:
- the **direct route** to Trient via Le Peuty described as the main Stage 2;
- **Alternative Stage 2** via Refuge Les Grands; and
- a slightly **longer option** (2hrs 15mins) by way of L'Arolette, Catogne and Les Tseppes – described in the boxed section at the end of this Stage.

Veer left beyond the refuge to a signpost at a footpath junction, then branch right to begin the descent. Trient is 2hrs from the col. The path goes down in long loops at first (a water supply at the hut of Les Herbagères), but once you enter forest the way steepens with tighter zig-zags. It brings you into a rough pastureland where you bear left to cross the Nant Noir stream and walk down to

LE PEUTY (1328m, 5–5¼hrs) self-catering (meals in Trient) gîte accommodation and camping at Refuge du Peuty, 37 places, open mid-June to mid-September (Tel 027 722 09 38 or Tel 079 217 12 62).

Continue down the road for a further 10mins to the village of

TRIENT (1279M, 5–5¼ HRS)

A small village set in a narrowing of the valley of the same name below La Forclaz. In spite of its being the first Swiss community met on this walk, it is nevertheless very French in both architecture and atmosphere. Its location is ideal for tackling the crossing of either the Fenêtre d'Arpette or Col de la Forclaz and Bovine route for the next stage to Champex.

The little village of Trient is the first in Switzerland

Dortoir accommodation at Auberge Mont Blanc, 70 places, small food store (limited opening times) open all year (Tel 027 767 15 05, **www.aubergemontblanc.com**); and La Grande Ourse, 38 dortoir places, 18 beds, open all year (Tel 027 722 17 54, **www.la-grande-ourse.ch**); PTT, Postbus link with Martigny. Tourist information: **www.trient.ch**.

If you have difficulty finding accommodation here, try Hotel du Col de la Forclaz 3km uphill to the east; 40 places in bedrooms and dortoir (Tel 027 722 26 88, **www.coldelaforclaz.ch**).

ALTERNATIVE DESCENT
FROM COL DE BALME TO TRIENT VIA L'AROLETTE

This descent to Trient from Col de Balme is slightly longer, a little more demanding, but more scenically interesting than the standard direct route described above.

Arriving at Col de Balme walk past the refuge and 1min later, where the path forks with the direct route to Trient branching right, continue ahead. The path curves round the hillside and forks again. Take the right branch, which rises gently and, 30mins from the refuge, brings you onto the 2330m saddle of L'Arolette to gain a view ahead of the distant Emosson dam backed by Mont Ruan.

The path now descends the north side of the pass, sweeping down and across the steep grass flank of the Croix de Fer. On coming to a signed junction at 2110m above the alp buildings of Catogne, fork right on a path which contours across pastures and into larchwoods with a view across the Trient gorge. The way turns a spur into the Trient valley, from where you look through the length of the upper valley to the Aiguille du Tour flanked by the glaciers of Trient and des Grands.

The descent into the valley takes you briefly into forest, then you gain another, but even better, view of the same mountain and its glaciers. About 5mins later pass the two timber chalets of Les Tseppes (1932m), and shortly after re-enter forest for a steep, knee-crunching descent. At another junction within the forest (1750m) bear left, and 20mins later come onto a track which you cross directly ahead to continue the descent. The same track is rejoined lower down, but once again you cross directly ahead onto a raised footpath that brings you onto the track once more. Follow this to the right, pass some chalets, cross a river and come onto a road at the upper part of **TRIENT** (2hrs 15mins from Col de Balme). For accommodation in the village bear left. For Col de la Forclaz take the upper road.

ALTERNATIVE STAGE 2
*Argentière – Col de Balme –
Les Grands – Col de la Forclaz*

Start	Argentière (1251m)
Distance	15km
Time	6½–7hrs
High point	Col de Balme (2204m)
Height gain	953m
Height loss	676m
Map(s)	LS 5027T Grand St Bernard–Combins–Arolla 1:50,000 or LS 282T Martigny 1:50,000
Accommodation	Col de Balme (3hrs) – refuge
	Les Grands (4½hrs) – refuge
	Col de la Forclaz – hotel, dortoir
Transport options	Bus (Argentière–Le Tour)
	Gondola and chairlift (Le Tour–Charamillon–Les Grandes Otanes near Col de Balme)

This alternative stage is a very scenic one, giving close views of glaciers and distant views of crowding mountains and hinted valleys. The first section as far as Col de Balme is the same as that used by the main Stage 2, but thereafter the ways diverge, with this alternative taking a variante of the TMB which passes a small self-catering refuge. It does not always have a guardian in residence, so should you plan to stay there it would be wise to carry food. A steep descent below Refuge Les Grands brings you to a bridge over the torrent draining the Glacier du Trient, followed by a lovely path alongside a *bisse* (an irrigation channel) to the hotel on Col de la Forclaz. A splendid day's walk.

Follow directions to Col de Balme as set out in Stage 2 above. This will take 3–3½hrs. A few paces before reaching the Chalet-Refuge bear slightly right at a footpath junction signed to Les Grands, Chalet du Glacier and Col de la Forclaz. The path contours for about 5mins, then descends a little along the right-hand hillside; in places the trail is narrow, but clear throughout. Having descended a short way it resumes a hillside traverse with views down to Trient and Col de la Forclaz.

About 40mins from Col de Balme, and having crossed a rocky section, the path turns a spur to gain a view into the upper reaches of the Trient valley and across to the Fenêtre d'Arpette. Now the hillside is

Refuge du Col de Balme on the Franco/Swiss border, after a summer snowstorm

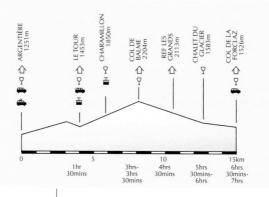

ARGENTIÈRE 1251m	LE TOUR 1453m	CHARAMILLON 1850m	COL DE BALME 2204m	REF LES GRANDS 2113m	CHALET DU GLACIER 1583m	COL DE LA FORCLAZ 1526m

0	5	10	15km
	1hr 30mins	3hrs-3hrs 30mins	4hrs 30mins	5hrs 30mins-6hrs	6hrs 30mins-7hrs

On the path to Refuge Les Grands, a good view is had of the Glacier du Trient

clothed with bilberry and alpenrose, and as the way advances so the path climbs again, with the Glacier du Trient seen ahead, and the smaller Glacier des Grands above to the right – superb alpine scenery. Topping a high point at about 2150m the Refuge Les Grands can be seen below. The path descends directly to it.

REFUGE LES GRANDS (2113m, 4½hrs) 15 places, cooking facilities, water supply; guardian sometimes in residence, open mid-June to mid-October; reservations (Tel 026 660 65 04)

The path descends directly below the hut, quite steeply in places, and soon slants across a rock face with fixed cable for safety. It then resumes in steep zig-zags, passes a couple of small ruins and enters pinewoods. On coming to a fork in the path ignore the right-hand option (which leads to Alpage des Petoudes) and continue ahead, eventually reaching another path junction by a footbridge spanning a glacial torrent. (If you plan to stay in Trient bear left here – the village is about 50mins downvalley.)

Cross the bridge to another path junction. A few paces to the right **CHALET DU GLACIER** (1583m) offers refreshments. The path which continues beyond it leads to the Fenêtre d'Arpette. We, however, turn left alongside the Bisse du Trient on a charming near-level path to reach in another 50mins

COL DE LA FORCLAZ (1526M, 6½–7HRS)

The path from Chalet du Glacier to the col was originally laid with rails in order to transport ice from the Trient glacier to the hotel on the pass. As for the road which crosses Col de la Forclaz, thereby linking Martigny with Chamonix, this was built between 1825 and 1887. The first motor vehicles crossed in 1912, with a maximum approved speed of 18km per hour – none were allowed to make the journey by night. In 1864 Edward Whymper came across the Forclaz and was constantly bothered by what he called 'parasitic children' who pestered him and other travellers on the road. 'These children swarm there like maggots in a rotten cheese,' he wrote. 'They carry baskets of fruit with which to plague the weary tourist. They flit around him like flies; they thrust the fruit in his face; they pester him with their pertinacity. Beware of them! – touch not their fruit... It is to no purpose to be angry; it is like flapping wasps – they only buzz more.'

Accommodation at Hotel du Col de la Forclaz, 40 places in rooms and dortoirs (Tel 027 722 26 88, **www.coldelaforclaz.ch**), camping, refreshments, shop

STAGE 3

Trient – Fenêtre d'Arpette – Champex

Start	Trient (1279m)
Distance	14km
Height gain	1386m
Height loss	1199m
Time	6½–7½hrs
High point	Fenêtre d'Arpette (2665m)
Map(s)	LS 5027T Grand St Bernard-Combins-Arolla 1:50,000 or LS 282T Martigny 1:50,000
Transport options	Postbus (Trient–Col de la Forclaz–Martigny) Train (Martigny–Orsières) Bus (Orsières–Champex)
Accommodation	Arpette (6hrs) – hotel/dortoir, camping Champex – hotels, pensions, dortoirs, camping

The crossing of Fenêtre d'Arpette is a classic outing and one of the most demanding of the whole walk. The approach to it is full of interest, with the frozen cascades of the Glacier du Trient's icefall in view nearly all the way, while the descent into the lovely pastoral Val d'Arpette begins with a wilderness of scree and boulders, but finishes with joyful streams, spacious woods and meadows. These contrasts are bound to bring pleasure to all Haute Route trekkers, for it is in such contrasts that long-distance mountain routes gain much of their appeal.

The path is a good one practically all the way, but care should be exercised on the initial descent from the pass where scree then boulder fields are crossed. A twisted ankle here could have serious consequences.

At the end of the day Champex is the first 'real' Swiss village of the route, with attractive chalets facing the sun and boxes of flowers at the windows. It's a popular, welcoming little resort that has grown along the shores of a small reedy lake, and is noted for its magnificent alpine garden – considered by many to be the finest in Switzerland.

An alternative approach to Champex, which is less demanding than the Arpette crossing, yet still a very pleasant walk in its own right, is the so-called 'Bovine' route, also adopted by the Tour of Mont Blanc. In suspect weather it would be preferable to the crossing of Fenêtre d'Arpette, and is described as Alternative Stage 3 below.

Above the church in Trient walk up the main Col de la Forclaz road to a sign by a stone cross on the left which directs the way to the Sentier du Bisse-Glacier along a broad grass track rising in long easy loops. At a junction of tracks continue ahead to regain the road. Cross directly ahead onto the continuing track which soon narrows to a footpath, zig-zags again and comes to a lovely *bisse* path where you turn right. (A *bisse* is an irrigation watercourse.) Follow this path all the way to the **CHALET DU GLACIER** (1583m, 1hr 20mins, refreshments). ▸

The path forks at the Chalet du Glacier. Bear left and climb uphill to another fork. Once more take the left branch (the right-hand, lower, path goes to the glacier), where the climb to the pass begins in earnest, first among woods, then above these on a more open stretch with clear uninterrupted views onto the fast-receding glacier. As you gain height so the Aiguilles Dorées and Pointe d'Orny grow above you to the south.

The gradient steepens, but the path is always clearly defined, even when crossing rocky slopes. Few paths allow such detailed study of an icefield in all its tortured glory as this does, and views are consistently magnificent. But the pass remains a well-kept secret until you're almost there.

A last scramble over a jumble of rocks brings you finally to the **FENÊTRE D'ARPETTE** (2665m, 4–4½hrs). This wild and rocky cleft makes a splendid pass, for the ridge it

Walkers who spent the night at the Hotel du Col de la Forclaz and plan to use the Fenêtre d'Arpette route should cross the road in front of the hotel where a signpost directs the path as Bisse du Trient – 50mins to the Chalet du Glacier.

STAGE 3: TRIENT – ARPETTE – CHAMPEX
ALTERNATIVE STAGE 3: TRIENT – BOVINE – CHAMPEX

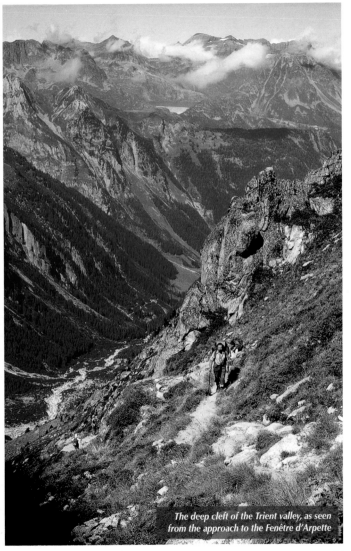

The deep cleft of the Trient valley, as seen from the approach to the Fenêtre d'Arpette

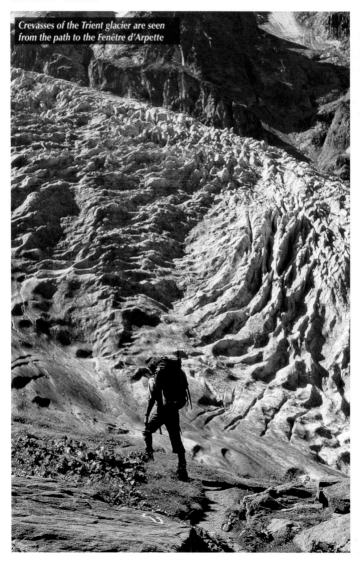

Crevasses of the Trient glacier are seen from the path to the Fenêtre d'Arpette breaches is very much a division; to the west all mountains and glaciers owe allegiance to Mont Blanc, while to the east lies a new world – a stony world rather than an arctic one, and it will be three more days before you again feel the brush of glacial air on your face. The three-day intermission goes from bare rocks to pasture and forest through a neat and tended landscape, a brief respite before the high mountains are regained. The Fenêtre d'Arpette is a geological hyphen, and from it you gaze eagerly to the east and south-east, where an array of ridges jostle the horizon and the Combin massif gleams a splash of white against the sky – a promise of good things to come.

We reached the pass in time to eat our lunch, emerging from a cool wind to bright sunshine and sun-warmed rocks on the Arpette side. But the walking world had come to the Fenêtre too, for everywhere we looked tanned bodies were spread across the rocks like basking seals. Not for nothing is this pass known locally as the Champs d'Elysées. Thank the popularity of the Tour of Mont Blanc for that, for the pass is on a much-loved TMB Variante. Ten thousand people a year walk that circuit. How was I to know they would all be gathered that very day on the Fenêtre d'Arpette?

This classic, scenically spectacular **Tour of Mont Blanc** makes a circuit of the Mont Blanc massif by way of the seven valleys that surround it. The TMB has numerous *variantes*, but the standard route is some 190km long and takes 10–12 days to complete. With some justification it is one of the most popular long-distance routes in Europe. See *Tour of Mont Blanc* by Kev Reynolds (Cicerone Press).

At first the descent drops into a rough, stony bowl at the head of Val d'Arpette. Caution is advised for the initial 100m or so where each one of an assortment of paths is particularly steep and, at times, loose under foot. Below this you cross a chaotic boulder field before the path (waymarked over the boulders) treats you with more respect and eases into Val d'Arpette proper.

Pastures and fruiting shrubs are a welcome relief after the barren rocks of the upper valley, and in almost 2hrs from the pass you come to a group of farms where a track leads onto the right bank of the stream. Five minutes later you reach the

RELAIS D'ARPETTE (1627m, 6hrs) 90 places in beds & dortoir, camping, refreshments, open from June to end-September (Tel 027 783 12 21, **www.arpette.ch**).

Just beyond the hotel turn off the main track/road and take a footpath on the left that descends among trees and follows a stream. On coming to a bridge cross over, then go right on a footpath waymarked with yellow diamonds and occasional green stripes. Recross the stream and soon after bear left when the path forks.

The fast-running brook you now accompany is a leat, or *bisse* – a watercourse created to direct part of a stream into a new valley, or to bring water to otherwise dry farmland. The Valais region has many such watercourses. One was followed at the start of the day, and there will be several more to follow in the days ahead. The path eventually brings you out of the woods at a small pond by a chairlift station. Go onto the road and bear right into

CHAMPEX (1466M, 7HRS)

Also known as Champex-Lac to emphasise its lakeside position, this modest-sized village has developed as an all-year resort. During the summer there's swimming in a heated pool, boating and fishing in the lake. The alpine garden (*Jardin Alpin Florealpe*) above the village on the hillside to the north contains more than 4000 plants, and is generally reckoned to be the finest collection in Switzerland.

Accommodation (hotels, pensions, dortoirs, camping), restaurants, shops, PTT, bus link with Orsières and Martigny. Tourist Information: **www.champex.info**. Lower-priced accommodation: Pension En Plein Air, 61 places in dortoirs & beds, open mid-Jan to the end of September (Tel 027 783 23 50, **www.pensionenpleinair.ch**); Au Club Alpin 25 dortoir places, open Jan to mid-November (Tel 027 783 11 61, **www.auclubalpin.ch**); Au Rendez-vous (b&b), 6 places open all year (Tel 027 783 16 40).

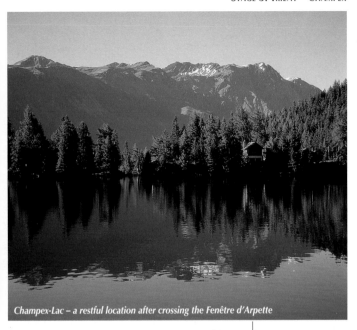

Champex-Lac – a restful location after crossing the Fenêtre d'Arpette

Arriving in Champex late in the afternoon we sought dortoir accommodation and were soon booked in at the Plein Air, to find surprisingly up-market comfortable beds in a dormitory with curtains dividing the room to allow a degree of privacy not normally experienced in such places. I went for a shower and came out at the same time as a Dutchman whom we'd met the previous evening in Trient. We both had wet towels and socks to dry so went onto the balcony outside our room to hang them out overnight. As we stood there, suddenly the balcony floor gave way beneath us and crashed onto the pavement, leaving the Dutchman and me hanging from the rail high above the street. We were wondering how to swing back into our room in safety when a shout from below caught our attention. It was a German trekker who'd also been in Trient the previous night. 'This looks good,' he called, waving his camera. 'Hold it there, I would like a photo of this.'

ALTERNATIVE STAGE 3
Trient – Col de la Forclaz –
Alp Bovine – Champex

Start	Trient (1279m)
Distance	16km
Height gain	929m
Height loss	710m
Time	5½hrs
High point	Above Alp Bovine, 2040m
Map(s)	LS 5027T Grand St Bernard–Combins–Arolla 1:50,000 or LS 282T Martigny 1:50,000
Transport options	Postbus (Trient–Col de la Forclaz–Martigny)
	Train (Martigny–Orsières)
	Bus (Orsières–Champex)
Accommodation	Col de la Forclaz (45 mins) – hotel, dortoir, camping
	Alp Bovine (2½hrs) – emergency dortoir only
	Champex d'en Haut (4½hrs) – auberge/gîte, hotel
	Champex – hotels, pensions, dortoirs, camping

This route is the bad-weather alternative to the more demanding Fenêtre d'Arpette crossing, but it should not be assumed that it is an uninteresting walk. Far from it. It's a green and pleasant way, among forest and pasture and with good views down into the Rhône valley and across to the Bernese Alps that rise on the northern side. Since this is the path of the main TMB (the Fenêtre route is a variante) it is well used, but the vast majority of walkers will be coming towards you.

From the church in Trient walk up to the main Col de la Forclaz road and bear right along it. Look for a sign on the left to Sentier du Bisse-Glacier by a stone cross. A broad grass track swings up the hillside in easy loops, and at junctions you follow signs for Col de la Forclaz (soon leaving the *bisse* route), and eventually the track brings you onto the road where a path runs along its left-hand side. After several hundred metres a sign directs you across the road and up a grass slope to

COL DE LA FORCLAZ (1562m, 45mins)
Accommodation at Hotel du Col de la Forclaz; 40
places in rooms and dortoirs (Tel 027 722 26 88,
www.coldelaforclaz.ch), camping, refreshments,
shop.

Immediately over the col on the east side just
beyond the shop, a sign to Alp Bovine points the way
along the edge of a meadow beside buildings, then
progresses on the top edge of a sloping pasture before
twisting in and out of woodland and gaining height with
views into the Rhône valley. Working a way round the
Combe des Faces, in about 1½hrs come to a junction
of paths (1725m) where you continue ahead, still rising
across the wooded hillside.

After about 1hr 45mins the way passes to the left of
a group of alp buildings (**LA GIÈTE** 1884m) in an open
grass basin, beyond which the path resumes in larch-
and pinewoods. Shortly after a short contouring section
that gives direct views onto Martigny, the trail rises to a
high point (2040m) on the edge of woodland from which
the buildings of Alp Bovine can be seen a short distance
ahead. The way now eases down the slope to reach

ALP BOVINE (1987m, 2½hrs) refreshments, emergency accommodation only

Alp Bovine, snug among its pastures

The alp buildings are just to the left of the path in a gentle slope of pasture with views north-east along the Rhône valley. The official trail (also used by the TMB) now descends slightly from Alp Bovine, and continues to zigzag down to Plan de l'Eau, while the original path contours towards the east, then curves south along the hillside before crossing a minor stream and descending steeply into more woodland.

The rough sloping pastures of La Jure (with excellent bilberries in late summer) are crossed about 50mins beyond Alp Bovine, then you descend an open slope to a track which eases round the hillside and brings you to the farm buildings of **PLAN L'EAU** (1330m, 3hrs 50mins, refreshments) which has a small buvette. From here the track becomes a narrow metalled road, but 2mins beyond the farm you break off to the right on a signed path which rises to woodland.

When the path forks in the forest take the left branch. Soon pass below a group of chalets and come to a road at **CHAMPEX D'EN BAS** (1299m, 4hrs 10mins). Turn right, pass the strung-out houses of this little village and at the upper end continue straight ahead at a minor crossroads. In 4½hrs come to

CHAMPEX D'EN HAUT (1440m) Accommodation at Auberge-Gîte Bon Abri, 77 dortoir places, open all year (Tel 027 783 14 23, **www.gite-bonabri. com**); Hotel-Club Sunways (Tel 027 783 11 22, **www.sunways.ch**).

About 300m beyond Hotel Sunways join the main valley road and turn right, rising to a high point at 1498m, then sloping downhill with the snow-crowned Grand Combin seen ahead, and come to

CHAMPEX (1466m, 5½hrs) Accommodation (hotels, pensions, dortoirs, camping), restaurants, shops, PTT, bus links with Orsière and Martigny. Tourist information: **www.champex.info**. Lower-priced accommodation: Pension En Plein Air, 61 places in dortoirs & beds, open mid-June to the end of September (Tel 027 783 23 50, **www. pensionenpleinair.ch**); Au Club Alpin, 25 dortoir places, open all year (Tel 027 783 11 61, **www. auclubalpin.ch**); Au Rendez-vous (b&b) 6 places, open all year (Tel 027 783 16 40).

There is ample accommodation in Champex

STAGE 4
Champex – Sembrancher – Le Châble

Start	Champex (1466m)
Distance	13km
Height gain	104m
Height loss	749m
Time	3½–4hrs
Low point	Sembrancher (717m)
Map(s)	LS 5027T Grand St Bernard–Combins–Arolla 1:50,000 or LS 282T Martigny 1:50,000
Transport options	Bus (Champex–Orsières) Train (Orsières–Sembrancher–Le Châble)
Accommodation	Sembrancher (2 hours 45 mins) – hotels Le Châble – hotels, pension, b&b

Leaving Champex the route departs from that of the Tour du Mont Blanc and footpaths will be less busy. On this stage a gentle downhill walk followed by a pleasant valley stroll makes a good cushion between two rather strenuous days. Although there are no passes to cross and no big glacier-hung mountains close at hand, it is by no means a dull day, for the path takes you into an everyday working Switzerland – a Switzerland that rarely appears in tourist brochures, but which nevertheless is good to see. There are small farming communities along the way, patches of hillside being cultivated far from chocolate-box resorts, and all with a general air of pastoral well-being.

If you were so inclined, Le Châble could be reached in a stiff morning's walk. But there's little to gain by rushing, for the onward route to Cabane du Mont Fort is too far to be achieved on top of this stage. Take the opportunity to enjoy a leisurely amble down to Sembrancher, and from there stroll into Val de Bagnes and make the most of your time.

Wander through Champex village heading south-east alongside the lake, and at the far end take the road branching left, signed to Hotels Belvedere, Splendide and Alpina. Rounding a dog-leg bend you come to the end of the road at Hotel Alpina. A few paces beyond the hotel at a junction of paths, take the right-hand option, signed to

STAGE 4: CHAMPEX – LE CHÂBLE

Sembrancher. Descending into woods it loses height with a steady gradient. Keeping straight ahead at all junctions you will come onto a gravel track which takes you above the hamlet of **CHEZ LES REUSE** (1158m).

Do not descend to the hamlet but continue straight ahead, joining another track coming from the right and soon cutting into a cleft above a small gorge. When it forks take the lower, right-hand branch which goes round pastureland, and you will come to another fork, where this time you take the left-hand option. Before long come to a T-junction of trails; bear left and 15m later slant away to the right on a waymarked grass track signed to Sous la Lé, La Garde and Sembrancher. This brings you down to a gravel farm road above the small village of **SOUS LA LÉ** (Soulalex on the map).

Walk down to the village, and then bear left at a water trough and wander along a narrow street that leads to a junction of roads where you continue straight ahead, but instead of descending to a group of houses, take the left-hand track signposted to La Garde (25mins from here). Keep to the main, upper track when a choice is given, until a second track junction is reached immediately after crossing a partially hidden stream. Ignore

Quiet villages on the descent to Sembrancher

that which cuts off left and continue ahead, now easing downhill among pastures to a junction of four tracks (**TETOU**). Go straight ahead on a path descending among trees, branching left at an intersection, and soon arrive in the village of **LA GARDE** (900m, 1hr 15mins).

In the village pass a chapel on your right and walk along a street in the direction of St-Jean and Sembrancher, then down to a crosstracks (**LE CREUX**) where you go straight ahead, soon reaching a hairpin bend in a road. Once more continue ahead on a track again signed to St-Jean and Sembrancher, following power lines. Between here and Sembrancher there are various footpath alternatives, with directions indicated at all route junctions. Perhaps the most direct trail is that which passes to the left of the little chapel of St-Jean and descends through woodland, goes beneath a railway line and brings you into the centre of

SEMBRANCHER (717m, 2–2½hrs) accommodation, refreshments, shops, PTT, Postbus and railway. Office du Tourisme (Tel 027 785 11 14).

Standing at the junction of Vals d'Entremont and Bagnes, Sembrancher is a stone-walled village with an attractive little square, which makes a good base for a

VAL DE BAGNES

Rising in an attractive cirque of mountains rimmed by the Swiss/Italian border south-east of the Grand Combin, the Val de Bagnes contains a diverse set of landscapes: from open tarn-flecked pastures to deep gorge-like defiles, and from bleak screes and seemingly barren moraines to forests and meadows full of flowers. There are several remote mountain huts, challenging trails and a number of walkers' passes, all of which make this a splendid base for a walking holiday – see *Walking in the Valais* by Kev Reynolds (Cicerone Press). Despite the fact that the valley is sparsely populated with only a few hamlets and even fewer villages, the Val de Bagnes commune is Switzerland's largest, and at 295km^2 is greater in extent than the cantons of Geneva, Schaffhausen and Zug.

The village square in Sembrancher

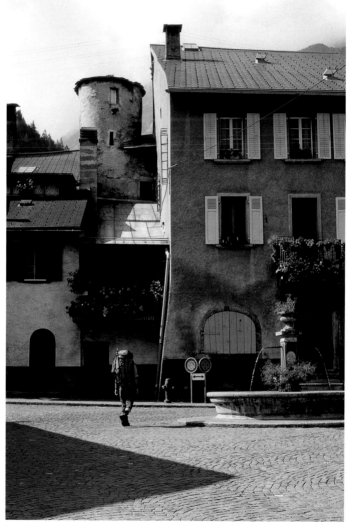

walking holiday since it has access to two appealing valleys and frequent public transport facilities. ▶

Leave the village by walking upvalley on the road heading into Val d'Entremont, signed (rather perversely) to Champex and Ferret. After 200m head left on a side road marked to Chamoille. Passing houses cross the river (la Dranse d'Entremont) and go straight ahead where the road forks at **LES MOULINS** (729m). The narrow tarmac road goes between low-lying pastures and fields with encouraging views ahead. When you come to a fork near a wooden cross take the left branch ahead. At another fork near a small fenced building, take the right branch on what is now a track, and wander up into forest.

Having gained height in the forest the track forks. Take the lower option, signed to Le Châble, and soon after break off on a waymarked footpath descending to the left. At the foot of the slope come onto a track at a hairpin bend. Go round this hairpin to the left and onto another track – the Promenade de la Dranse. Wander ahead

The signed path from the water fountain misses the centre of Sembrancher and avoids walking on the main road. It crosses the main road and leads directly onto the side road signed Chamoille.

Looking ahead to Le Châble and the mountains ahead on Stage 5

alongside the Dranse de Bagnes, eventually coming to a narrow metalled road near a bridge. Do not cross the river but follow the road between meadows to enter

LE CHÂBLE (821M, 3½–4HRS)

Huddled on the left (west) bank of the Dranse de Bagnes, Le Châble is the valley capital, while its neighbour just across the bridge on the east side of the river is the more modern 'suburb' of Villette. Le Châble's village square has a very French appearance, but some of the old stone-walled farmhouses in the back streets pronounce their Valaisian authenticity by displaying over their doorways the horns of long-deceased cattle that have taken part in cow fights (*Combats de Reines*), a purely local (Valaisian) tradition. Cable-car access with Verbier starts just across the river next to the railway station – Le Châble is the valley terminus of a branch line of the St Bernard Express which begins in Martigny. From the village a twice-daily Postbus service runs upvalley (July–Sept only) as far as the huge Mauvoisin dam, from where walkers and climbers set out on a 4hr trek to the Chanrion hut.

Accommodation, restaurants, shops, banks, PTT, Postbus & cableway to Verbier, train to Martigny. Office du Tourisme, 1934 Le Châble (Tel 027 776 16 82, **www. verbier.ch**). Lower-priced accommodation: Hotel La Poste (Tel 027 776 11 69); and in Villette across the river: Hotel du Gietroz (Tel 027 776 11 84), Restaurant L'Escale (Tel 027 776 27 07) and Hotel La Ruinette (Tel 027 776 13 52).

STAGE 5
Le Châble – Clambin – Cabane du Mont Fort

Start	Le Châble (821m)
Distance	9km
Height gain	1636m
Time	6–6½hrs
High point	Cabane du Mont Fort (2457m)
Maps	LS 5027T Grand St Bernard–Combins–Arolla 1:50,000 or
	LS 282T Martigny & 283T Arolla 1:50,000
Transport options	Postbus (Le Châble–Verbier)
	Cableway (Le Châble–Verbier–Les Ruinette)
Accommodation	Cabane du Mont Fort – SAC refuge

A first glance at the map gives little indication that a walking route can be made between Val de Bagnes and Cabane du Mont Fort without extensive use of either the steeply twisting road to Verbier or the lengthy zig-zag road from Lourtier through Sarreyer.

But there is a route, and a delightful one at that. It's a combination of narrow lanes, tracks and footpaths – often steeply climbing, but always interesting. There are some fine villages, an attractive chapel, long forest sections with welcome shade on a hot day, high pastures and some truly magnificent views. With so much height to gain it is advisable to make an early start, take your time and enjoy everything the ascent has to offer. But before setting out you should telephone ahead to reserve bed-space for the night at Cabane du Mont Fort – the number is given at the end of the route details.

This walk avoids Verbier altogether in an effort to remain as far from mechanisation as possible. It's impossible to escape all sign of the downhill ski industry, however, for Verbier and its surrounding hillsides offer a winter paradise for the skier, and an abundance of lifts and cableways have effectively laced the mountains like an old-fashioned corset. Whilst one deplores such desecration, thanks must be offered that a wholesale sacrifice has not been made to the transitory thrill of downhill skiing, that there are still ways for the wanderer to escape and that even here paths may be found that mostly ignore pylons, cables and bulldozed pistes.

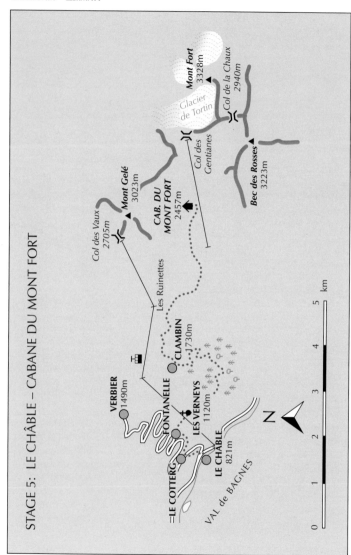

STAGE 5: LE CHÂBLE – CABANE DU MONT FORT

It is on this stage that the Grand Combin begins to exert its influence. This great snowy massif dominates the Val de Bagnes (and, to an extent, Val d'Entremont too). It's the most westerly 4000m mountain of the Pennine Alps, an attractive, substantial block that cultivates a number of glaciers and whose presence is recognised for several days yet to come. Although the walk does not stray to it, the Combin nevertheless imposes its personality on the Haute Route trekker with its sheer size and grandeur. Since leaving Mont Blanc (whose bulk was always behind you) the Combin massif is the first on the walk to impress with such authority and grace.

▶ From Le Châble cross the river to **VILLETTE** and bear left. (Initially the route is part of the Tour des Villages, and is waymarked with yellow diamonds or stripes outlined in black.) Bear right past Café-Restaurant La Ruinette and follow waymarks up through the village along narrow streets, passing houses and dark timber granaries, some of which are perched on staddle stones. In 10mins cross the Villette–Verbier road by Café Magnin and enter **LE COTTERG** (880m). A signpost directs you to the right to Chapelle les Verneys in 50mins (ignore the sign to Cabane du Mont Fort, for this goes via Verbier), and with waymarks and signposts as your guide, a series of tracks and footpaths lead to **LA FONTANELLE**.

As you come to this hamlet, dug into the steep hillside, take a narrow footpath breaking away beside a wooden cross (dated 1982) to edge alongside an orchard (1045m, 30mins). An unmetalled road takes you round the hillside heading south-east, and eventually brings you to the small but elegant white chapel and few buildings of **LES VERNEYS** (1120m, 1hr, water supply, public toilets).

Continue beyond the buildings for about 5mins, and when the track makes a sharp right-hand bend, take a signed footpath ahead leading uphill. This goes into forest, gaining height steeply at times in order to cross a scoop in the mountainside. This 'scoop' opens to a combe higher up. Crossing a stream the way climbs on, but having gained a high point you then descend a few metres to a junction of paths (1200m, about 25mins from Les

Should you decide that the steep uphill route to Cabane du Mont Fort is not for you, an easy option is to take the cableway from Le Châble to Verbier, and from there to Les Ruinettes at 2195m. From there a signed track-then-path leads to the Mont Fort hut in 1hr 10mins.

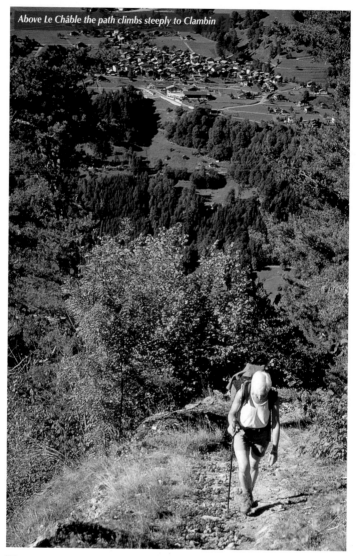

Above Le Châble the path climbs steeply to Clambin

Verneys). Turn left, rising once more in forest on a path signed to Les Ruinettes and Clambin, with yellow and black waymarks.

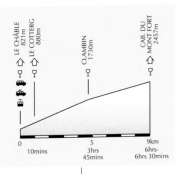

This trail rises quite steeply on the right-hand (south) side of what soon becomes a distinctive combe and leads to a handful of timber buildings, above which you bear left on an unmetalled road, and when it forks soon after, take the upper track. This winds uphill in long loops with waymarked footpath short-cuts.

The footpath leads up to a pair of wooden buildings (**LA COMBE** 1555m) and passes between them. A few paces beyond these the path forks (this may not be very clear). Take the lower option across the hillside combe, enter forest and continue for some way to a footpath junction at 1600m, where you bear right on a rising trail signed to Clambin and Les Ruinettes. (The path straight ahead at this junction goes to Verbier.) It's a steep ascent, but when you come out of forest to a small open patch of pasture, there's a wonderful view of the Combin massif on the far side of Val de Bagnes. This is the first of many magnificent sightings, but the magic never fades.

THE COMBIN MASSIF

The large and impressive Combin massif has several distinct summits over 4000m. Standing entirely in Switzerland the summit crown has a splay of ridges from which busy glacial systems pour down; the largest being the great Glacier de Corbassière which falls in a series of terraces to the north, and is the largest icefield in the Western Pennine Alps. (A fine close view of these icy terraces is to be had from Cabane de Pannoissière, reached by a 4hr walk from Fionnay.) Although several ascents were made of a secondary peak (Aiguille du Croissant) in 1857–58, the actual summit of Grand Combin (Combin de Graffeneire, 4314m) was first climbed on 30 July 1859 by Charles St-Claire Deville, with the guides Daniel, Emmanuel and Gaspard Balleys and Basile Dorsaz. Nowadays the massif attracts ski mountaineers as well as summer-season climbers, and is frequently traversed by those tackling the winter Haute Route on ski.

Continue towards a stone-based chalet, but veer left before it and pass beside a timber chalet with Verbier seen below in a large grassy basin. An easy path then brings you to a junction of tracks at **CLAMBIN** (1730m, 3hrs 45mins, refreshments) – an attractive restaurant which enjoys a wonderful panorama is seen a short distance to the left. There's a water supply nearby. Go right, then immediately left on a track signed to Les Ruinettes and Cabane du Mont Fort.

VERBIER

One of the best-known ski resorts in the Alps, Verbier sprawls within a large natural basin of hillside high above the valley, a real sun-trap and an obvious site for development as a ski village since the amphitheatre that cradles it holds plenty of snow and the slopes are ideal for skiers of all standards. It has an over-abundance of mechanical lifts – 80 or so, if you include those in the neighbouring Val de Nendaz which is easily accessible from it. Thanks to the great ski boom of the 1960s, the original village of Verbier has been swamped by a rash of chalets, hotels and unattractive apartment blocks, but many footpaths lead from it to take the eager walker into scenes of peace and tranquility. For information contact: Office du Tourisme, 1936 Verbier (Tel 027 775 38 88, www.verbier.ch).

This track rises to another junction (**HATAY** 1844m), where you bear right and a few paces later slant left uphill and come to a picnic/barbecue area marked as **LE HATTEY** (1860m, water supply). A broad piste has been bulldozed down the hillside above Le Hattey, but the path crosses and recrosses this, climbing still in forest until emerging at last to spectacular views of the Grand Combin and the Mont Blanc massif beyond intervening ridges in the south-west.

On coming to a track by a cableway pylon (5hrs 15mins from Le Châble) turn right along it. Before long this rises as a path, and at a signed junction continues alongside a *bisse* to a dirt road. Cross this road to another narrow path which rises in a few paces to join another *bisse*. There are wonderful views still to Grand

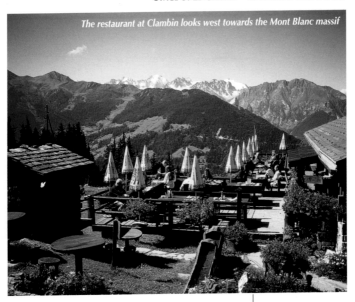

The restaurant at Clambin looks west towards the Mont Blanc massif

On this upward path we came upon an elderly Swiss couple descending. They wore smiles as bright as their red shirts and were so obviously enjoying their day out that we stopped to speak and shared with them a love of the morning, of the near views and far, and talked briefly of other mountains and valleys, of huts and villages, of glaciers and snowfields and birdsong and the fragrance of the forest – in general feeding off each other's enthusiasm. Then the lady whispered that her husband could now only walk up the gentlest of hills – but he'd swallowed his pride and taken the occasional chairlift or cable-car to enable him to reach the loftier viewpoints from which he was happy to walk down. 'Well,' she confided, 'he is 82.' With that my prejudices stacked against cableways in the mountains came crashing down around me.

Combin and its neighbouring peaks and glaciers drawing you on. Follow the *bisse* path on an easy contour round the hillside leading to a junction of trails below the knoll on which stands

Cabane du Mont Fort

CABANE DU MONT FORT (2457m, 6–6½hrs) 58 places, meals and drinks available (Tel 027 778 13 84, **www.cabanemontfort.ch**). Owned by the Jaman Section of the Swiss Alpine Club, this hut is superbly placed on a bluff due south of Mont Gelé and is understandably popular with C–Z trekkers (advance booking advised). There are several high passes within easy reach, including Col de Chassoure, Col du Mont Gelé, Col des Gentianes, Col de la Chaux and Col Termin, which are all crossed by walkers in summer. Unfortunately a spider's web of cableways has devalued some of these passes, but others happily remain free from mechanisation. Despite ski lifts and farm tracks below, views from the hut are splendid, with Grand Combin and the Mont Blanc massif taking pride of place, but the Dents du Midi are also on show. Sunsets are magnificent.

STAGE 6

Cabane du Mont Fort – Col Termin –
Col de Louvie – Col de Prafleuri –
Cabane de Prafleuri

Start	Cabane du Mont Fort (2457m)
Distance	14km
Height gain	885m
Height loss	740m
Time	6–6½hrs
High point	Col de Prafleuri (2965m)
Map(s)	LS 5027T Grand St Bernard–Combins–Arolla 1:50,000 or LS 283T Arolla 1:50,000
Transport options	None
Accommodation	Cabane de Prafleuri – mountain refuge

Before the present trek was established mountain walkers attempting to work out a traverse of the high country between Val de Bagnes and Val des Dix often sought ways to avoid the Grand Désert glacier draped down the northern flanks of Rosablanche. Alternative passes were tried, and long circuitous routes taken via the lower reaches of Val de Nendaz. But as the Grand Désert shrank back, so its crossing became fairly straightforward. For several years there were no major crevasses to worry about, and unroped walkers could tackle the ice without concern.

Then the glacier changed and a potentially dangerous crevasse opened up which made this crossing impractical for most walkers. But the continuing speedy withdrawal of this glacier makes a diversion below the ice more appropriate, so the present route drops below the glacier snout to a small lake, followed by an uphill slanting walk over rocks and screes to regain the original route.

The stage is full of variety and ever-changing views. At first there are vast panoramas, but as you wander along the high belvedere trail to Col Termin, so the Combin massif dominates the scene, and if you walk quietly and remain alert, you stand a good chance of seeing ibex on or near the path. (This is a noted wildlife sanctuary.) Later, on the eastern side of Col de Louvie, you are faced with a bewildering landscape of dying glaciers, chaotic moraines and a seemingly barren wilderness. But even in such landscapes the majesty of the mountains impresses itself; yet one grows convinced (if you ever needed convincing) that the 'everlasting hills' are everlasting only in the words of the poet. On this walk you are witness to the ceaseless toil of erosion. The mountains are dying, falling apart, and to wander through their scenes of destruction is a sobering experience.

Under normal summer conditions the walk should present no major route-finding difficulties, but in poor visibility, or under threat of storm, problems may arise on the stretch between Col de Louvie (2921m) and Col de Prafleuri (2965m), where there is no real path other than a trail of cairns and paint flashes. The Sentier des Chamois between Cabane du Mont Fort and Col Termin is also one to avoid under certain bad-weather conditions. Seek the advice of the guardian at Mont Fort in case of uncertainty. He may advise crossing Col de la Chaux as a safer option – this is described as Alternative Stage 6 below.

The following route is a long and tiring stage – remember that the time quoted (6–6½hrs) does not include rests of any kind, so it could take at least 8–9hrs to get from one hut to the next. Fill your water bottle before setting out, and make sure you have food to sustain you on what could be the toughest day of the walk so far.

Descend north-east from Cabane du Mont Fort to the major path junction where you turn right, and after a few metres branch left on a red–white waymarked path that winds downhill to meet a track at a hairpin bend. Follow the track to the next (right-hand) hairpin, then break away on a narrow path heading across a basin of rocks and scree. It crosses a few minor streams, then makes a rising traverse of the slope ahead, where you turn a spur which marks the start of the Sentier des Chamois. With

STAGE 6: CABANE DU MONT FORT – CABANE DE PRAFLEURI
ALTERNATIVE STAGE 6: VIA COL DE LA CHAUX

The Combin massif, seen from the Sentier des Chamois

splendid views of the Combin massif, the *sentier* is narrow and exposed in places, but it makes a tremendous belvedere as you contour along the precipitous mountainside high above the Val de Bagnes.

In a little over an hour from the hut you reach a junction where a trail descends to Le Mintset. Ignore this and continue straight ahead, but keep alert for signs of ibex or chamois. Views remain magnificent – Grand Combin aloof across the valley, and the Val de Bagnes itself a very long way beneath the trail. Views back to the north-west show the Dents du Midi in the distance.

We were finding the path difficult to negotiate. Not that there were obstacles in the way, nor were conditions at all bad. Neither were we bothered by the steep slopes plunging to Val de Bagnes 1500m below. Our problems arose from lack of concentration, for the glories of the Combin massif across the valley were so outstanding that our attention was being held by them – away from the first principle of safety on the path. It was difficult to take our eyes off that gleaming mass that had conjured a streamer of cloud just below the summit and was teasing as in a dance of the seven veils. The summit was clear, so were the lower slopes. But the midriff of the mountain was veiled. It was a tantalising view. Then, when we did correct our attention to review the way ahead, it was to spy a herd of twenty or so ibex moving unconcerned in morning shadow below us. They were very close, and completely unconcerned by our presence.

The way then reaches the saddle of **COL TERMIN** (2648m, 1hr 40mins) in a shoulder of the Bec Termin which rises to the north. From here a very wild landscape rises to north and east, with Mont Fort and Rosablanche both casting out some high ridges to confuse.

Rosablanche (3336m) offers easy ascent routes and a celebrated panorama from its summit – an exceptionally fine viewpoint from which to study larger peaks of the main Pennine chain. It is popular as a skiing expedition in spring, and from the Prafleuri hut for walkers in summer (2hrs from the hut by way of the Prafleuri glacier). It was first climbed in September 1865.

Descend on the east side for a few metres, then veer sharply left on the path signed to Col de Louvie and Prafleuri. (Steeply below lies Lac de Louvie, with a refuge above its southern end that enjoys one of the finest views in the Swiss Alps; worth remembering for a return visit to Val de Bagnes.) About 15mins from the col another path breaks away and descends to the lake, but you ignore this and continue towards a wild-looking rocky cirque at the head of the Louvie valley. A rough boulder tip is crossed, but after this the path improves. Views remain impressive.

An hour from Col Termin you reach a path junction where the left-hand option breaks away to Col de la Chaux and Mont Fort (Alternative Stage 6). Continue straight ahead, over a second boulder field and, skirting the left-hand side of a narrow stony valley (good waymarks and a clear path), you climb to gain the rocky **COL DE LOUVIE** (2921m, 3hrs 15mins).

A barren landscape greets you in the north-east – a wilderness of screes, moraine and the dying glacier spilling from Rosablanche. The Grand Désert is well named.

Descending from the col the way hugs the left-hand side of a narrow, rocky little valley – again, well waymarked, although care is needed in places where there is no real path. As you lose height note a large red–white

Lac de Louvie nestles in its combe with the Combin massif as a backdrop

Both the LS 1:50,000 and Kummerley + Frey 1:60,000 maps show an old path passing south of the tarn, which is no longer in use.

waymark painted on a boulder on the eastern side of the valley ahead, beyond the Grand Désert glacier – this is a guide for later. Follow the immediate line of waymarks and occasional cairns that lead down to the outflow stream at the northern end of a glacial tarn (2760m, 3hrs 50mins) below the snout of the Grand Désert. Over this turn right and make your way initially south-east, then north-east up and across a vast stony wasteland to a line of cairns and waymarks. ◄

The route takes you past a number of little tarns and glacial ponds, crossing broad granite slabs and jumbled boulders. Waymarks are frequent, but in poor visibility it is absolutely essential not to lose sight of them. Take compass bearings where necessary.

Col de Prafleuri is seen at the head of what looks like a steep slope of scree. A small glacier flows down from Grand Mont Calme west of the pass, and the way-marked trail brings you to its edge, where it is neces-sary to descend a short but steep and broken slope (sometimes snow or ice) in order to continue to the foot of the pass. Descend with care – a frustrating descent, for you have to climb again to reach the pass.

The climb to the col can be tiring, as it involves working a way up a steepish slope of rough blocks, scree and scattered rocks, but at last (and no doubt with relief) you arrive at the **COL DE PRAFLEURI** (2965m, 5½–6hrs) to be greeted by a view south-east over a much-scarred and depressingly barren mountain bowl to Mont Blanc de Cheilon, which dominates much of Stage 7.

Descend the steep path winding down to a level section beneath the Glacier de Prafleuri. Cross levelled gravel beds to a track where you bear right, soon leaving this on a waymarked footpath that drops to the left into a grim-looking valley with a first sighting of Cabane de Prafleuri. The path takes you below the hut, so that the final approach is unfortunately up a short but steep path that deposits you at the doorway of

CABANE DE PRAFLEURI (2662m, 6–6½hrs) 59 places, manned from mid-March to end of April, and early July to mid-Sept, with a full meals service (Tel 027 281 17 80, **www.prafleuri.ch**). Privately owned, the original Cabane de Prafleuri was constructed in the mid-1950s when quarrying work began below the Prafleuri glacier as part of the Grande Dixence hydro-electric scheme. (The hut was used to house site-workers in the early days.)

Cabane de Prafleuri, a privately owned hut with excellent facilities

While it lacks any views of inspiration, it is particularly well sited for walkers on the Chamonix–Zermatt route, for immediately above it to the south the easy Col des Roux gives access to Val des Dix. Ibex often approach the hut in the evening. (There is also a bizarrely ugly but functional hotel at the foot of the Dix Barrage, 1hr from Prafleuri.)

ALTERNATIVE STAGE 6
Cabane du Mont Fort – Col de la Chaux –
Col de Louvie – Col de Prafleuri –
Cabane de Prafleuri

Start	Cabane de Mont Fort (2457m)
Distance	10km
Height gain	885m
Height loss	740m
Time	5½hrs
High point	Col de Prafleuri (2965m)
Map(s)	LS 5027T Grand St Bernard–Combins–Arolla 1:50,000 or LS 283T Arolla 1:50,000
Transport options	None
Accommodation	Cabane de Prafleuri – mountain refuge

On this more direct, and therefore slightly shorter route to Col de Louvie, the Col de la Chaux is seen behind Cabane du Mont Fort at the head of a stony hanging valley. Although it is rough underfoot and without the wonderful views of the Sentier des Chamois – Col Termin main route described in the previous section, the Col de la Chaux crossing is preferable and safer under certain conditions. Should the guardian at Cabane du Mont Fort advise against using the Sentier des Chamois, this could be your best bet. Check locally for current conditions. Comments at the head of the previous section with regard to the route from Col de Louvie to Col de Prafleuri apply also to this Alternative Stage.

Descend from Cabane du Mont Fort on an easy-angled track that winds into the stony basin to the east. As you enter the basin/hanging valley, note that there are two tracks pushing into it. Go to the upper track and follow this as it pushes upvalley, curving in long loops to gain height. After about 45mins come to a junction (2706m). The continuing track climbs to Col des Gentianes, but the Col de la Chaux path breaks away to the right.

The path, waymarked red–white, picks a way across a very stony terrain and passes above a small glacial lake. It then steers onto the left-hand slope of the hanging valley, guided still by waymarks and cairns where the path is thin or non-existent. Near the head of the valley a very large waymark painted on a rock below the col ensures you keep left of the shrinking Glacier de la Chaux.

So gain the rocky **COL DE LA CHAUX** (2940m, 1hr 45mins) to exchange one desolate stony scene for another. Looking back you see beyond the coffee-coloured glacial tarn to Cabane du Mont Fort and the spiky Dents du Midi as a backdrop. Ahead lies another stony bowl, and across its bounding ridge the summit of Rosablanche can be seen with the Grand Désert glacier draped down its north-west face.

A steep descent path cuts left below the col, skirts the slopes of the basin then veers right (well waymarked)

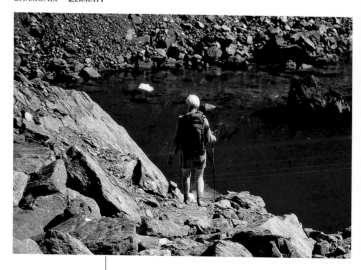

The trail from Col de la Chaux to Col de Louvie skirts this small tarn, still carrying ice in September

to cross a rocky shoulder from which the Grand Combin is once more on show. Here you find a junction of paths at 2840m (2hrs 15mins). That which descends ahead goes to Col Termin, while the left-hand path leads to Col de Louvie.

Take the Louvie path across ribs of rock and boulders, then descend to the right of a glacial tarn to join another path where the letters T, L and C are painted on a rock (T = Termin; L = Louvie; C = Chaux – the three col destinations). Take the left-hand option which rises as a good path to gain **COL DE LOUVIE** (2921m, 2hrs 45mins). Both the Mont Blanc massif and Grand Combin can be seen when looking back from here.

For the continuing route to Cabane de Prafleuri, see Stage 6 above.

STAGE 7

*Cabane de Prafleuri – Col des Roux –
Col de Riedmatten – Arolla*

Start	Cabane de Prafleuri (2624m)
Distance	16km
Height gain	735m
Height loss	1353m
Time	6½hrs
High point	Col de Riedmatten (2919m)
Map(s)	LS 5027T Grand St Bernard–Combins–Arolla 1:50,000 or LS 283T Arolla 1:50,000
Transport options	Bus (Le Chargeur–Vex) Postbus (Vex–Arolla)
Accommodation	Refuge des Ecoulaies (50mins) – mountain refuge Refuge de la Gentiane la Barma (1hr) – mountain refuge Arolla – hotels, dortoirs, camping

The walk that leads from the rather gloomy Prafleuri glen to Arolla is a true delight. Given fine weather conditions the views on this stage will be among the very best of all. There's the surprise vision that greets you on arrival at the first col of the day (Col des Roux), for you emerge from morning shadow to the incredible sight of the Val des Dix spread before you – a 5km lake, green pastures and big mountains. Best of all these mountains is the great pyramid-shaped Mont Blanc de Cheilon; but it has its handsome neighbours too, and as the day progresses so you draw closer to them, crossing Col de Riedmatten to descend beside Pigne d'Arolla, then below Mont Collon. Col de Riedmatten is a revelation – a rocky cleft in the Monts Rouges ridge from which you have a first view of the Matterhorn far off. (Make the most of it for you'll not see it again until you approach Zinal on Stage 10.)

With two passes to cross, and some taxing sections on the approach to Col de Riedmatten, this stage is more demanding than it was before the route was diverted and a landslide reshaped part of a hillside. But by now you should be well into your stride and able to pace the first half of the walk in comfort. On arrival at Col de Riedmatten, the beauty of the scene before you will put any weariness into perspective.

Alternative Stage 7 described below also makes a very fine trek, with the opportunity to break the walk with an overnight spent in Cabane des Dix, set dramatically below the great north face of Mont Blanc de Cheilon. Both routes have much to commend them, but the Col de Riedmatten crossing is the more direct.

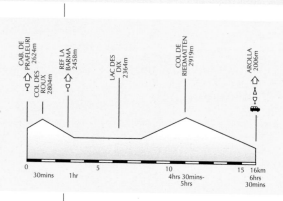

A signpost outside Cabane de Prafleuri indicates the start of the route to Col des Roux. There are also large painted signs on rocks and, where no actual path exists, sufficient waymarks keep you on track. Col des Roux is an obvious pass seen to the south of the hut and only 180m above it. The route is by way of a slope cluttered with rocks, but after an initial boulder tip, a good path leads to the col in easy zig-zags. In fact the ascent is achieved quickly and a lot more easily than might be imagined from below, and you come onto **COL DES ROUX** (2804m) in about 30mins, to be rewarded by a view almost guaranteed to stop you in your tracks.

On the south side descend on a good trail that brings you to more boulders but then becomes easier under foot. As you veer south-westward into the pastures of a shallow valley below the Glacier des Ecoulaies, you can see the solitary building of the

STAGE 7: CABANE DE PRAFLEURI – AROLLA
ALTERNATIVE STAGE 7: CABANE DE PRAFLEURI – CABANE DES DIX – AROLLA

CAB. DE PRAFLEURI 2624m

Col des Roux 2804m

REF. DES ECOULAIES 2575m

REF. LA BARMA 2458m

Lac des Dix

Gl. de Vouasson

AIGUILLES ROUGES D'AROLLA

Col de Riedmatten 2919m

Pas de Chèvres 2855m

AROLLA 2006m

Tête Noir
CAB. DES DIX 2928m

Gl. de Cheilon

Mt. Blanc de Cheilon 3870m

N

0 1 2 3 4 5 km

REFUGE DES ECOULAIES (2575m, 50mins), owned by the Ski Club des Pyramides (Euseigne). It has 22 places and is usually manned at weekends in summer; self-catering facilities only. For reservations Tel 079 339 12 46 (**www.lespyramides.ch**).

The waymarked path descends between two streams to the Dix track – for Ref La Gentiane, the path aims towards the refuge then forks. Take the left branch which crosses several streams, then descend to a glacial torrent with a footbridge. Over this the way eases round the hillside and brings you to another junction by the stone-built

Val des Dix and its lake appear as you gain Col des Roux, just 30 minutes above Cabane de Prafleuri

REFUGE DE LA GENTIANE LA BARMA (2458m 1hr). This privately owned hut is permanently open, but not always manned. It has places for about 30 and self-catering facilities. For enquiries and/or reservations contact: the Sté de Gymnastique 'La Gentiane' – A Nendaz (Tel 027 281 27 93) or C Pralong (Tel 027 281 18 82). If you do use the facilities, please treat them with respect and do nothing to abuse the hospitality offered.

Overlooking Lac des Dix the privately-owned **Refuge de la Gentiane La Barma** was originally part of a cheese dairy built in 1934 alongside cowsheds. When the dairy was abandoned in 1964, the buildings were acquired by the Gymnastic Society, La Gentiane, of Mâche (downvalley in Val d'Hérémence), which renovated them to create this delightful 30-place refuge.

The descent from Col des Roux gives a view of the Glacier des Ecoulaies

Take the path ahead which passes just to the left of the refuge, and cross a meadow to join a farm track which you follow downhill to a hairpin bend. A signed path strikes ahead, then descends to a broad track running along the west side of Lac des Dix. Bear right and walk upvalley. With little effort required you can swing along with all senses alert to the wonders of the day, with marmots whistling from the trackside pastures, the clang of cowbells matching your stride, streams spilling down the hillsides, and snowgleam topping the peaks ahead.

The track alongside Lac des Dix makes for easy walking, in contrast to the later approach to Col de Riedmatten

LAC DES DIX

Created as part of the Grande Dixence hydro-scheme that harnesses the waters of several Valaisian valleys, Lac des Dix is blocked at its northern end by the massive dam known as the Barrage de la Grande Dixence. At 284m the dam is claimed to be the world's highest. It's an impressive piece of engineering; from its base to the crest of the wall it stands twice as tall as the largest of Egypt's pyramids. It consists of 5,960,000m³ of concrete and holds back some 400 million m³ of water. The Grand Dixence scheme has a number of dams, all linked by service tunnels and feeder pipes.

About 20m before the track ends at a point known as the **PAS DU CHAT** (2371m, 2hrs 15mins), a sign indicates a path climbing steeply to the right. This mounts a slope of grass and rock, and continues for some time, climbing relentlessly before easing to the start of a rib of lateral moraine. The path ascends this moraine where you come to a signpost at about 2630m (45mins or so from the Pas du Chat) directing the Col de Riedmatten/Arolla route to the left. (The way to Cabane des Dix continues along the moraine crest.)

The shapely **Mont Blanc de Cheilon** (3870m) dominates the Val des Dix and towers over Cabane des Dix. Generally reckoned to be the finest peak in the Arolla district for rock and ice routes, it received its first ascent in September 1865 by the west-north-west flank, which is reached from the Col de Cheilon. (This is the usual route today, and the one most often used in descent.)

▶ Go down the left-hand path and in another 5mins you cross a footbridge over the stream draining the Cheilon glacier, which is receding at an alarming rate. The way now cuts across glacial silt and moraine debris, then winds up the rock-strewn slope towards the Col de Riedmatten and Pas de Chèvres. Waymarks guide you up the slope to a point where red paint announces the way to the Pas de Chèvres (the ladders seen to the right). But for the Col de Riedmatten fork left and climb an unrelentingly steep slope to gain the narrow notch of **COL DE RIEDMATTEN** (2919m, 4½–5hrs) and a window onto a new world.

In poor visibility this is a tricky area – do not allow yourself to be misled by the blue signs to the difficult Col des Ignes. Also do not follow the signs to the Dix hut. You have gone too far if you do so.

The final climb up the gully to the col can be aggravated by loose grit and requires some effort. An alternative is to break off to the right at the foot of the gully and follow waymarks to the ladders of the Pas de Chèvres. There are four near-vertical ladders bolted to the rockface – not to be attempted by anyone suffering vertigo – at the top of which a path descends on the eastern side of the ridge to join that from Col de Riedmatten.

Trading shadows for sunshine on my first crossing of the col we gained that rocky cleft and light suddenly flooded ahead, washing a land of snow, ice, rock and a distant slope of grass. Below, the ridge fell into a basin of mountain-ejected debris, but our eyes were uninterested in any of this, for our attention was held by the crest of Pigne d'Arolla, by the great iced gateau of Mont Collon, by the sharp stiletto blade of the Matterhorn's upper reaches far off, by a vast wall of rock notable for the little spire of the Aiguille de la Tsa projecting from it, and by the snow-wrapped Dent Blanche on the far side of that wall.

The narrow cleft of the Col de Riedmatten is a gateway to a new world

PIGNE D'AROLLA AND MONT COLLON

An easy snow mountain that neighbours Mont Blanc de Cheilon to the east, the Pigne d'Arolla is often ascended by ski mountaineers during a spring traverse of the classic Haute Route. An outstanding viewpoint, from it can be seen in one vast panorama most of the mountains of the Pennine Alps that feature on the Chamonix–Zermatt route, as well as the chain of the Bernese Alps. The Gran Paradiso and other peaks of the Graian Alps are also visible, and it has been claimed that the Mediterranean can be detected from the summit on a clear day. The first ascent was made by AW Moore, Horace Walker and their guide, the 'fearless' Jakob Anderegg, in July 1865. At 3796m, it's a distinctive peak recognised from afar.

More than any other, Mont Collon is the dominant feature of the Arolla valley (the upper south-western arm of Val d'Hérens). Despite its modest altitude (3637m), the rocky buttresses, snow domes and apparent bulk give this mountain an imposing stature out of all proportion to its true size. Glaciers flow round its east and west flanks like icy calipers, effectively giving Mont Collon the appearance of an island peak, but to the south it is attached to the higher L'Evêque by way of the Col de la Mitre. Mont Collon was first climbed by GE Foster with H Baumann and J Kronig in 1867. There are several routes of varying grades adorning its face, pillars and ridges today.

Descending to the east the path is clearly defined although rather steep at first. It leads into an undulating bowl of grassland where it then veers to the right and joins another path coming from the Pas de Chèvres (crossed on Alternative Stage 7). Curving left to head east the path, clear and undemanding, takes you easily down towards Arolla. Mont Collon disappears from view, but Pigne d'Arolla grows in stature on the right with the long Tsijiore Nouve glacier carving its way in a deep trench behind a grass-covered wall of moraine. Then, as you approach Arolla, so Mont Collon reappears like an island in a sea of ice.

The path divides two or three times, but you simply follow the waymarked trail all the way down to

AROLLA (2006M, 6½HRS)

This small mountaineering centre and minor ski resort was one of the first to be 'adopted' by the British. In 1921 the skeletons of a man and a chamois, along with a rifle and coins dating from before 1850, were revealed by a shrinking glacier. Attractively set among woods of larch and Arolla pine, Arolla is slowly expanding, but it remains one of the smallest villages on the Walker's Haute Route. As a base for a mountaineer's first alpine season it takes a lot of beating, while it also makes a very fine walking centre. (See *Walking in the Valais*, Kev Reynolds, published by Cicerone Press, for ideas.)

Accommodation (hotels, pension, dortoir), camping, restaurants, shops, postbus link with Les Haudères and Evolène. Further information from: Office du Tourisme, 1986 Arolla (Tel 027 283 10 83, **www.arolla.com**). Lower-priced accommodation: Chalet Edelweiss, 40 dortoir places (Tel 027 283 23 12); Chalet Les Ecureuils, 28 places (Tel 027 283 14 68, **www.arolla-bazar.ch**); Chalet Le Sporting, 47 dortoir places – below Arolla (Tel 027 283 17 06 or 027 398 39 38, **www.latza.ch**); Hotel de la Tza, beds and 64 dortoir places – 10mins below Arolla (Tel 027 283 14 06, **www.latza.ch**); Hotel du Glacier, beds and dortoir places (Tel 027 283 12 18); Hotel Kurhaus, beds and dortoir places (Tel 027 283 70 00, **www.hotel-kurhaus.arolla.com**); Hotel Mont Collon (Tel 027 283 11 91); Hotel du Pigne d'Arolla (Tel 027 283 71 00). Possible room(s) to rent – enquire at the village shop opposite the tourist office/post office. There is also pension (and dortoir) accommodation at the hamlet of La Gouille, 1hr 45mins further on – see Stage 8 for details.

The most direct route to the Hotel de la Tza is via a yellow waymarked path which begins on the right immediately before Hotel du Glacier. In 10mins this slopes easily down to the road directly opposite Hotel de la Tza.

ALTERNATIVE STAGE 7

Cabane de Prafleuri – Col des Roux –
Cabane des Dix – Arolla

Start	Cabane de Prafleuri (2624m)
Distance	17km
Height gain	837m
Height loss	1289m
Time	6½hrs
High point	Tête Noir (2981m)
Map(s)	LS 5027T Grand St Bernard–Combins–Arolla 1:50,000 or
	LS 283T Arolla 1:50,000
Transport options	None
Accommodation	Refuge des Ecoulaies (50mins) – mountain refuge
	Refuge de la Gentiane la Barma (1hr) – mountain refuge
	Cabane des Dix – SAC refuge (4–4½hrs)
	Arolla – hotels, dortoirs, camping

This alternative to the main route described above has much to commend it. It shares the first 2hrs or so of the Stage 7 route as far as the Pas du Chat, but then branches off to follow a moraine path to the Dix refuge, after which it then crosses the Glacier de Cheilon by a marked route to tackle the four vertical ladders of the Pas de Chèvres. In most summers the path across the Cheilon glacier is heavily used and should cause no disquiet, as crevasses are virtually non-existent at the point of crossing. As for the Pas de Chèvres, the ladders are securely bolted to the rock face, but some walkers find them intimidating. Since they are clearly seen as you approach them, it's easy for anyone who feels uneasy to divert to the Col de Riedmatten (as per Stage 7).

Cabane des Dix occupies a truly spectacular site with a direct view onto the north face of Mont Blanc de Cheilon, and makes an ideal site for a lunch stop. It is, however, an extremely busy hut, and all intending to use it for overnight lodging are urged to telephone in advance.

Follow Stage 7 route directions as far as the **PAS DU CHAT** (2371m), about 20m before the track is blocked at the southern end of Lac des Dix (2hrs 15mins). Take the path on the right, which climbs over slopes of grass and rock. The way continues heading south to reach the foot of a rib of lateral moraine, then climbs to a signed junction (about 45mins from the Pas du Chat). Ignore the left-hand option to Col de Riedmatten, and keep along the moraine rib. The path is clear and views ever interesting, and as you make progress along it so you can see the deep col of Pas de Chèvres on the far side of the glacier.

Towards the end of the moraine the path veers right, descends into the ablation valley, then rises over grass slopes and onto screes by which you gain the north-west shoulder of the Tête Noir, which hides not only Mont Blanc de Cheilon, but also the Cabane des Dix.

As you rise towards the saddle on this shoulder, a wonderful panorama is seen off to the left (east). Far beyond the Monts Rouges ridge a jagged collection of peaks holds your attention. In that collection is the Matterhorn, whose profile from here is quite different to that normally seen from Zermatt. It appears as a distant stiletto with a marked shelf projecting to the south just beneath the summit. Then, when you gain the saddle, the vast pyramid of the north face of Mont Blanc de Cheilon appears before you, while the hut can be seen below, perched on top of a rocky knoll. The path winds

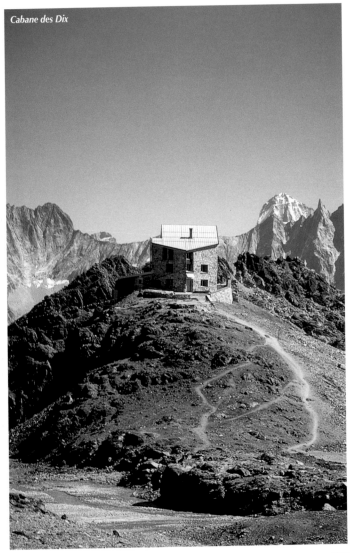

Cabane des Dix

down into a glacial plain, crosses a stream or two, then strikes directly up the slope to reach the

CABANE DES DIX (2928m, 4–4½hrs) 120 places, restaurant service, fully staffed from mid-March to end of May, and from July to mid-Sept (Tel 027 281 15 23, www.cabanedesdix.ch, advance booking essential). Owned by the Monte Rosa section of the Swiss Alpine Club, this refuge is one of the busiest in the Alps and is used by walkers, climbers and ski-tourers alike.

From Cabane des Dix descend the knoll on a clear path that winds leftwards (south) to the edge of the rubble-strewn Glacier de Cheilon, and then head north-east across it. Marker poles, cairns and waymarks give directions. It's an easy crossing with practically no crevasses, but it is important to follow the precise line shown by the markers.

On reaching the far side continuing waymarks and cairns steer you slanting left towards the base of Col de Riedmatten (crossed on Stage 7). As it negotiates a chaos of rocks and boulders, this section can be quite tiring. On gaining a clear path coming from Lac des Dix and leading to Col de Riedmatten, bear right, and a few

Climbing the ladders to the Pas de Chèvres – now given a safer (but uglier) alternative

paces later the path forks. The left branch climbs to Col de Riedmatten, while the right-hand path goes to the ladders of the Pas de Chèvres.

This latter path tucks against the base of the ridge, and traverses beneath it with long sections of fixed chains as far as the foot of the ladders. Of the four, the third is the longest, but each one is near vertical and securely attached to the rock face. Care, however, should be exercised – especially when carrying a large rucksack. One or two rungs are so close to the rock face that only the toes of your boots can gain purchase, and at the top of the third ladder it is necessary to step to the right onto a flat rock before climbing the final one. (In 2014 safety platforms were added.)

So reach the **PAS DE CHÈVRES** (2855m) about 1hr 15mins from the refuge. A very fine panorama now unfolds, which includes the Veisivi–Bertol wall above Arolla, with the delicate little Aiguille de la Tsa projecting from it, and beyond that the top of Dent Blanche, summit cone of the Matterhorn, Mont Collon and many more. It's a col to relax on and enjoy before tearing yourself away to tackle the descent.

Between the Pas de Chèvres and Arolla, the path is flanked by snowpeak, glacier and old moraine walls

An easy path takes you down on the eastern side, at first quite steeply, into a basin of rough grassland to join the path of Stage 7 coming from the neighbouring Col de Riedmatten. The walk down towards Arolla follows a clear trail, much trodden by walkers and climbers. On the right Pigne d'Arolla towers in a sweep of rock and ice, with the long Tsijiore Nouve glacier bulldozing a huge trough behind a grass-covered moraine wall. Views are consistently lovely.

Simply continue down the path, which forks two or three times above the village; however, all paths lead to Arolla unless otherwise signed. The final approach is through pleasant woodland, and about 6½hrs from Prafleuri you arrive in

AROLLA (2006m). See Stage 7 for accommodation details.

STAGE 8

Arolla – Lac Bleu –
Les Haudères – La Sage

Start	Arolla (2006m)
Distance	10km
Height gain	215m
Height loss	554m
Time	4hrs
Low point	Les Haudères (1452m)
Map(s)	LS 5027T Grand St-Bernard-Combins-Arolla and 5028T Monte Rosa–Matterhorn both 1:50,000 or LS 283T Arolla 1:50,000
Transport options	Postbus (Arolla–Les Haudères–La Sage–Villa)
Accommodation	La Gouille (1hr 45mins) – pension, dortoir
	Les Haudères (3hrs) – hotels, camping
	La Sage – dortoir, hotel
	Villa (+ 15 mins) – simple rooms (self-catering only)

Although this is a short and reasonably undemanding stage, it is not really practical to go beyond La Sage (or Villa), as neither the crossing of Col du Tsaté nor Col de Torrent offers prospects of accommodation for at least another 5hrs. It is nonetheless a stage to enjoy for there are numerous features to brighten the way.

The route to Les Haudères by way of Lac Bleu is designed to avoid all but the very briefest sections of road walking, in addition to providing an excuse to visit one of the best-loved sites around Arolla. There are charming views when you gaze back the way you have come; there are woodlands and small meadows, but a few short exposed sections too, safeguarded with fixed chains or cables; and between Lac Bleu and La Gouille there's a small alp hamlet. From La Gouille a wooded path leads to some lovely old houses on the edge of Les Haudères, a mountaineering centre at the head of Val d'Hérens, where it forks into the tributary glens of Arolla and Ferpècle. Then, leaving Les Haudères, a steady rising traverse path ascends the hillside to La Sage.

BOOKING AHEAD

Before setting out on this stage it is advisable to telephone ahead to book rooms for the night as there's limited accommodation in both La Sage and Villa. Failure to secure beds in either of these places will necessitate a return to Les Haudères. If this should happen it might be worth taking an early postbus next morning to La Sage (for the Col du Tsaté route) or Villa (for the Col de Torrent option).

From Arolla to Zermatt the Walker's Haute Route is shared by the Tour of the Matterhorn, most of whose trekkers will be walking towards you. But their numbers could clearly have an impact on the amount of accommodation available. For details of this route, which crosses two crevassed glaciers on its 10-day circuit, see *Tour of the Matterhorn* by Hilary Sharp (Cicerone Press).

From the village square in Arolla walk down the side road towards Hotel du Glacier. About 40m before the hotel take a signed path on the left which climbs above chalets, then eases towards the red-shuttered buildings of the Centre Alpin. Go between the buildings and onto a footpath rising into woodland. ◄ On coming to a signed junction take the upper path (*Chemin.dificile* – direction Louché, Lac Bleu and La Gouille); the lower branch is an easier but less interesting path which also goes to Louché and Lac Bleu.

In bad weather, you can opt to descend through meadows beside the river in the valley bottom.

Climbing steeply at times, the path picks a way among alpenrose and juniper, and at the upper tree level crosses a stream just below a group of alp huts. Wandering across an open slope, with lovely backward views to Mont Collon and the Pigne d'Arolla, the path crosses more streams, then re-enters woodland after tackling the first of several slightly exposed sections protected either by fixed cables or chains.

The route develops into something of a switchback, an undulating trail that absorbs the natural line. After a very exposed section overlooking the hamlet of Satarma, cross a high point, then descend very steeply (caution when wet) to two footbridges. At the foot of the next steep descent the path forks – the lower branch being the alternative (yellow waymarked) path that offered an easier option from Arolla. Take the upper fork to cross

STAGE 8: AROLLA – LA SAGE

A backward glance from the trail to Lac Bleu shows Mont Collon and Pigne d'Arolla

two more streams before twisting uphill among larches. The continuing path contours, then climbs again to top a grass bluff overlooking the aptly named **LAC BLEU** (2090m, 1½hrs). Once again there's a fine view back to Mont Collon, although Pigne d'Arolla has disappeared at this point.

Go down to the tarn's outflow and along a footpath to a tiny alp hamlet (**LOUCHÉ**) where cheese and milk may be purchased. Just below the hamlet the path forks again. Branch right and descend a steep grass slope, then go through forest to reach the small hamlet of

LA GOUILLE (1844m, 1hr 45mins) Accommodation at Pension du Lac Bleu, 9 rooms and 28 dortoir places, meals and refreshments (Tel 027 283 11 66, www.hotelarolla.com); postbus to Les Haudères.

Bear left down the Arolla–Les Haudères road for about 200m, then slope off to the right on a path way-marked yellow and black. This eases along the hillside below the road and soon joins a track near the tiny white-painted chapel of St Barthélemy (1823m). Continue down

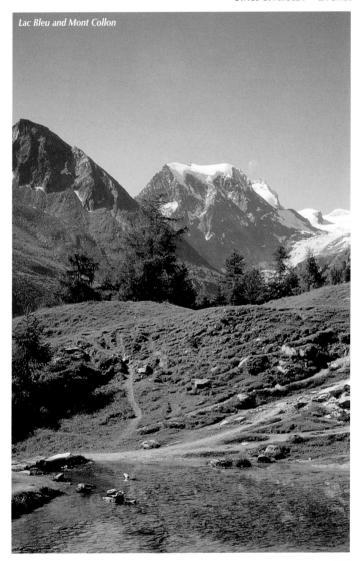

Lac Bleu and Mont Collon

the track, and when it forks wander straight ahead. With
gentle gradients the track leads downvalley and eventually comes to a group of handsome old timber houses. Just
beyond these join the main road, bear right and walk into

LES HAUDÈRES (1452M, 3HRS)

This attractive, unspoilt and typically Valaisian village is mostly contained in a
triangle delineated by two roads and a steep hillside at the head of Val d'Hérens.
Most of its buildings are of timber on a stone base, with granaries mingled among
the houses and small garden plots. Its houses are adorned with window boxes
bursting with flowers, while the granaries, or hay barns, are perched on staddle
stones to deter rodents. Les Haudères makes a good base for a walking holiday,
the two adjacent valleys (of Arolla and Ferpècle) being of special interest and
having superb high mountain views.

Hotels, camping, restaurants, shops, PTT, postbus. Office du Tourisme, 1984 Les
Haudères (Tel 027 283 10 15, **www.evolene-region.ch**). Lower-priced hotels:
Des Alpes, 16 beds (Tel 027 283 16 77); Les Mélèzes, 20 beds (Tel 027 283 11
55); Dents de Veisivi, 18 beds (Tel 027 283 11 01); Edelweiss, 38 beds (Tel 027
283 11 07); Garni Gai-Logis, 16 beds (Tel 027 283 14 13).

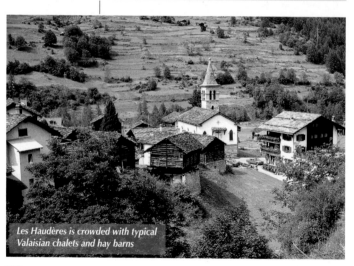

*Les Haudères is crowded with typical
Valaisian chalets and hay barns*

After crossing the bridge at the village entrance bear right on the road heading towards Ferpècle, La Forclaz and La Sage, but then turn left opposite Hotel des Alpes. Wander along a narrow street lined with attractive, typically Valaisian timber buildings, and follow through on an upper village street where there are both direction signs and waymarks.

It's an interesting stroll for it takes you past some of the oldest and best of Les Haudères's buildings, then above the village a track continues at the same steady angle, soon among trees. When it bends sharply to the right leave the track for a path continuing straight ahead. When this forks take the upper, right-hand path which leads between meadows and onto the road near La Sage.

Almost immediately take a narrow tarmac road on the left. It winds between pastures and brings you up a slope to pass Hotel de la Sage before coming onto the road in the middle of

LA SAGE (1667M, 4HRS)

This small village is built on a natural terrace some 250m above the valley, with charming views towards Pigne d'Arolla, or south-east to the snowfields and glaciers that spread between Dent Blanche and the Bouquetins ridge. A frequent postbus service travels between Les Haudères and the roadhead at Villa, passing through La Sage. As with several other villages in Val d'Hérens, local women often wear traditional long black dresses, decorated with colourful embroidery.

Accommodation, restaurant, shop, postbus. Office du Tourisme, 1985 La Sage (Tel 027 283 23 07, **www.lasage.com**). The central Tourist Information number for the area is Tel 027 283 40 00. Beds at Hotel de la Sage (Tel 027 283 24 20, **www.hoteldelasage.com**). 40 dortoir places at Café-Restaurant L'Ecureuil (Tel 027 283 24 55).

Limited (self-catering) accommodation is available at Villa the next village along the road, about 15mins from La Sage. Apply at the small shop as you enter the village or contact: Fam. Maurice Gaudin, 1985 Villa/La Sage (Tel 027 283 13 57).

STAGE 9

La Sage – Col du Tsaté – Cabane de Moiry

Start	La Sage (1667m)
Distance	10km
Height gain	1617m
Height loss	459m
Time	5–5½hrs
High point	Col du Tsaté (2868m)
Map(s)	LS 5028T Monte Rosa–Matterhorn 1:50,000
	or LS 283T Arolla 1:50,000
Transport options	None
Accommodation	Cabane de Moiry – SAC refuge

Between Val d'Hérens and Val d'Anniviers – the next major valley on the journey heading east – lies the small but lovely Val de Moiry, a tributary glen that feeds Anniviers. A long ridge system which maintains an altitude of 2900m and more extends north-westward from the Grand Cornier, making an effective divide between the Vals d'Hérens and Moiry, but with several accessible cols enabling walkers to cross from one to the other.

Col du Tsaté is the lowest and most direct of these crossing points for anyone staying in La Sage and planning to visit Cabane de Moiry, while Col de Torrent further north will be the choice of walkers aiming for either the dortoir at the Barrage de Moiry or Grimentz.

The rocky Col du Tsaté forms a break in the ridge linking Pointe du Bandon and the Couronne de Bréona, and although early Baedeker guides spoke of it as being 'toilsome' (an accurate description), there's nothing difficult about it – a long, steep walk over grass slopes with an upper stony basin just below the col, followed by an equally steep, but much shorter, descent on the eastern side.

Cabane de Moiry stands on a rocky knoll overlooking the Moiry glacier in such a spectacular position that all effort to reach it will be considered worthwhile. The final approach to it climbs along a wall of lateral moraine, followed by a steep zig-zag path up rocks. It's quite a demanding route, but a rewarding one, and from the hut one gains an amazing head-on view of the Moiry icefall. Of all lodgings on the Chamonix–Zermatt walk, this must rank among the finest for its setting.

From the centre of La Sage walk down the road in the direction of Les Haudères, and about 50m beyond Café-Restaurant L'Ecureuil bear left onto a tarmac lane rising into forest where it becomes a track. After passing a few alp buildings come to a junction of tracks, and bear left to continue rising in larchwoods. In another 2mins the track forks again. Curve right and in 25mins go round a left-hand hairpin. Shortly before reaching Moyens de Motau the track bends once more and you gain a view of the Ferpècle glacier, the top of the Dent Blanche and the rocky eminence of the Pointes de Veisivi. So come to the huddle of buildings of **MAYENS DE MOTAU** (1920m, 40mins, water supply), a small alp hamlet built on a steep open hillside enjoying fine views.

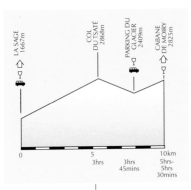

Above the hamlet the track stays close to a stream, narrows to a footpath which soon crosses to the left

The climb to Col du Tsaté passes through the hamlet of Mayens de Motau

STAGE 9: LA SAGE – CABANE DE MOIRY
ALTERNATIVE STAGE 9: LA SAGE – BARRAGE DE MOIRY

of the stream, then climbs again quite steeply alongside more larchwoods. After about 1hr 10mins come to another group of alp buildings, **LE TSATÉ** (2164m). Keeping left of these buildings continue uphill to cross a farm track, and climb on up the steep hillside on a narrow path which leads to a solitary hut just below another section of unmade farm road (1½hrs).

Veer left and slant up to the road, then cross to a continuing path which now climbs with more generous loops to gain height, before swinging to the right (south-east) and arriving at **REMOINTSE DU TSATÉ** (2480m, 1hr 50mins) – two long cowsheds and a small dairyman's hut. These buildings are situated at the entrance to a grass basin in which there's a small tarn, unseen from here. Immediately beyond the cowsheds turn right on a track, and a few paces later veer left (red–white waymarks) on a faint path across a little meadow. Cross a stream, then walk up to a lovely flowery meadow in which you can see the small unnamed tarn to your right (2502m).

Keep well to the left of the tarn and follow the path as it rises into a second basin where the way forks. Keep with the right-hand option, rising to a crucifix at the entrance to a third and final basin – this one much more austere and stony than the previous two, at the head of which is Col du Tsaté.

Passing just to the right of the crucifix the path crosses the stony bed of the valley, then rises on the left-hand walling hillside. As height is gained the way grows progressively more rocky until at last you emerge onto the summit of **COL DU TSATÉ** (2868m, 3hrs).

VAL DE MOIRY

This small glen of Val de Moiry feeds into the longer Val d'Anniviers, of which it forms the south-western tributary. It rises in a wedge of peaks whose nodal point is the Grand Cornier (3962m), and in whose upper ridges a basin of névé gives birth to the Moiry glacier. Below the glacier two small tarns are used as settlement reservoirs to reduce the flow of glacial silt into the larger dammed Lac de Moiry below.

Along the hillsides east and west of the lake a very fine path has been created more or less following the 2500m contour, and is promoted as the Haut Tour du Lac, from which the full extent of the valley is on display (a 5hr circuit). Below the Barrage de Moiry the glen is green and wooded towards Grimentz, an attractive village near the valley mouth and the only one in Val de Moiry. In summer a frequent postbus service runs between Grimentz and Parking du Glacier. At the barrage there's a restaurant, with a dortoir on the hillside above the east side of the dam.

The east side of the ridge which falls to the Val de Moiry is also stony at first, and the descent steep in places as it crosses screes and slopes of shale before coming onto a pleasant grass shelf (about 20mins below the col), from which you gain a first view of the Moiry icefall and refuge – the latter stands atop rock slabs to the left of the icefall. Continue down to a small tarn and a path junction at 2547m.

MOIRY GLACIER ICEFALL

The icefall of the Moiry glacier is among the most impressive of its kind in the Pennine Alps, and that the mountain walker can gaze upon it from so close and safe a vantage point as the hut makes it extra special.

In *The Alps in 1864*, the Victorian pioneer AW Moore wrote about it in glowing terms, referring to it as: 'a tremendous ice-fall of great height and very steep. The lower part extends completely from one side of the glacier to the other, but higher up, under the Pigne de la Lex, is a belt of smooth ice, which we had no doubt would give access to the field of névé above the fall. Below this great cascade of séracs, the ice is as compact and level as above it is steep and dislocated. Indeed, I never saw an ice-fall confined within such plainly defined limits, or terminate so abruptly.'

In order to continue to the Cabane take the path ahead, signed to Parking du Glacier. It descends in zig-zags, now with the dammed Lac de Moiry seen to the north, and eventually brings you to a track which swings down to the roadhead **PARKING DU GLACIER** (2409m, 3hrs 45mins) which has a small *buvette* (refreshment hut) and a bus stop for Grimentz.

The Haut Tour du Lac/Chemin 2500m makes a traverse left, and joins the route of Alternative Stage 9 at a farm, Alpage de Torrent. Should you have changed your mind about going to the Moiry refuge, you could follow this path to the farm, then descend to the Barrage de Moiry for overnight in a dortoir.

Pass to the left of the *buvette* onto a track signed to Cabane de Moiry. The track soon becomes a footpath which rises onto the east side lateral moraine walling

Cabane de Moiry, an atmospheric place in which to spend a night

For the adventurous, a path along the west side of the glacier gives access to a crossing directly to the refuge, but glacier conditions will change from year to year.

the Moiry glacier. ◀ After picking a way along the narrow moraine crest it slopes down into the little ablation valley before climbing in zigzags up rocky slopes which lead directly to the

CABANE DE MOIRY (2825m, 5–5½hrs) 100 places, fully staffed with meals provision from the end of June to end of September (Tel 027 475 45 34, www.cabane-de-moiry.ch).

CABANE DE MOIRY

Owned by the Montreux section of the Swiss Alpine Club, the Cabane de Moiry is built in a dramatic location among a horseshoe of peaks and glaciers. In 2010 the hut was extended with excellent new accommodation facilities and a magnificent glass-walled dining room overlooking the glacier.

Above it to the east runs the wall of the Aiguilles de la Lé; opposite rise Couronne de Bréona, Pointe de Moiry and Tsa de l'Ano. Between the Couronne and Pointe de Moiry lies the Col de Couronne, by which access to the glen may be achieved from the head of Val d'Hérens (a more strenuous and less well-marked route than either Col du Tsaté or Col de Torrent), while south-east of the hut, between the last of the Aiguilles de la Lé and Pigne de la Lé, Col du Pigne offers another way over to Zinal. (Not for inexperienced mountain walkers, though.)

The hut is popular among ski-mountaineers, for several of the summits that enclose the glacier provide enjoyable ski ascents. Pigne de la Lé and Pointe de Bricola (north-west of Grand Cornier) are among the most popular, while summer ascents are made directly from the hut to Grand Cornier and all the neighbouring peaks. By virtue of its short approach from the roadhead (1½hrs), Cabane de Moiry receives plenty of day-visitors.

ALTERNATIVE STAGE 9

La Sage – Col de Torrent –
Barrage de Moiry/Grimentz

Start	La Sage (1667m)
Distance	10km (16km to Grimentz)
Height gain	1252m
Height loss	670m (or 1347m)
Time	5hrs (7hrs to Grimentz)
High point	Col de Torrent (2919m)
Map(s)	LS 5028T Monte Rosa–Matterhorn 1:50,000
	or LS 283T Arolla 1:50,000 (& LS273T Montana for
	Grimentz option)
Transport options	Postbus (Barrage de Moiry–Grimentz)
Accommodation	Villa (15mins) – self-catering rooms
	Chalet du Barrage – dortoir
	Grimentz – hotels

A little over 4km north-west of Col du Tsaté (crossed on Stage 9 above) the higher Col de Torrent is a popular and much used link between the Vals d'Hérens and Moiry. Pastureland rises almost all the way to the col on both sides of the ridge, and views are consistently fine. The way up to the pass is a delight, while the panorama on the eastern side is the equal of almost anything seen so far, with the descent to the dammed Lac de Moiry being both undemanding and visually rewarding.

The dortoir above the barrage is ideally placed for the crossing of Col de Sorebois to Zinal next day, but some commercial trekking parties (and a few individuals) choose not to stay at the Chalet du Barrage, continuing instead down to Grimentz where there's a range of accommodation on offer. With this option the onward route misses Zinal completely by going directly to Hotel Weisshorn, thereby reducing the length of the walk by one day. Details of this option are given below.

Walk up the road from La Sage to **VILLA** (1714m, 15mins, accommodation, refreshments, shop, postbus to/from Les Haudères). Just across the bridge in Villa turn right opposite a small white chapel where a sign indicates the way to Mayens de Cotter, Col de Torrent, etc. Go alongside a granary, then turn right on a cobbled track that rises above the village. When the cobbles end, the track continues.

In 40mins the track forks by a stream. Keep ahead to the right side of this stream and 4mins later, when it makes a right-hand hairpin, leave the track to follow a path straight ahead, still along the right-hand side of the stream. The path then crosses the stream and angles up the hillside, and – climbing steadily – it then goes through a strip of larchwood and on to a footbridge and a junction of tracks. Walk ahead along a farm road, soon passing a few timber chalets, barns and a water supply.

From the outset views are very fine, not just to those peaks behind that have grown familiar from walking beside them during the past few days, but ahead too, to mountains of the Bernese Alps on the far side of the Rhône valley. Les Diablerets and the Wildhorn massif look especially appealing.

In 1hr 10mins turn a right-hand hairpin and continue to the group of farms and chalets of **MAYENS DE COTTER** (2057m) reached 5mins later, from which views show the Dent Blanche, Tête Blanche, Pigne d'Arolla and many other peaks. Immediately after passing a large farm building and a water trough, take a footpath cutting back to the left and rising across the steep grass hillside in long loops. This hillside is used by parapente enthusiasts, as evidenced by a number of windsocks.

The path brings you up to and past an upstanding pillar of rock, and beyond this curves to the right onto a grass rib that leads through a basin of pastureland in which there are a few semi-derelict huts (**BEPLAN**). In about 2hrs 25mins pass a little pond on your left (2536m) and a large cairn on your right. This is a splendid vantage point with an extensive view.

Beyond the pond the path continues to rise, making a long sweep to the east before cutting back to the left in order to make the final ascent to the **COL DE TORRENT** (2919m) in 3½–4hrs. There's a large wooden cross just to the right of the actual pass, and tremendous views. To south and west the panorama includes the Mont Miné, Tête Blanche, Grande Dent de Veisivi, Mont Brulé, Pigne d'Arolla, Mont Blanc de Cheilon, Grand Combin, the Aiguilles Rouges, Rosablanche and, far off, the snowy mass of Mont Blanc. Turning to the east across the lovely Lac des Autannes and jade-green Lac de Moiry, which

Pigne d'Arolla is clearly seen from the climb to Col de Torrent

Lac des Autannes makes a glistening foreground to views of the Moiry glacier

lie in the deep trough of Val de Moiry, stand Weisshorn, Schalihorn and Pointe Sud de Moming.

For an even **broader panorama** than that won from the col, go left up the ridge for 45mins (allow 1½hrs for the round-trip) to the summit of Sasseneire (3250m), where far to the north you can just make out the line of the Jura through the Col de Cheville, while to the south the Dent Blanche, which is not seen from the Col de Torrent, dominates the view.

A clear path descends on the Moiry side, first heading north, then swinging eastward down to undulating pastures. As you draw level with the picturesque **LAC DES AUTANNES**, some 230m and 15mins or so below the col, exquisite views are to be had across the tarn to a turmoil of glaciers and peaks that block the head of Val de Moiry. Up there, Pigne de la Lé, Grand Cornier and Dent Blanche cast ridges, snowfields and long streamers of ice, creating those contrasts of light and shade, height and depth, and barren upland against a foreground of soft pasture that make wandering in the Alps such a memorable experience.

Beyond the lake a good path descends rough pastures and brings you to a junction of tracks by the **ALPAGE DE TORRENT** (2480m, 4½hrs, water supply). The route of the Haut Tour du Lac breaks off to the right, but the way to the barrage continues ahead. Remain on this track all the way to the massive **BARRAGE DE MOIRY** (2249m) at the northern end of Lac de Moiry. Cross the dam to a restaurant on the eastern side (5hrs, refreshments, w.c., public telephone, postbus to Grimentz). For dortoir accommodation apply at the restaurant, then take the path which climbs the slope above the parking area to reach the

> **CHALET DU BARRAGE** (2300m, 5hrs) also known as the Gîte de Moiry, it has 24 dortoir places, self-catering facilities, but meals at the restaurant, open June to end of September (Tel 027 475 15 48, **www.moiryresto.ch**).

Continuing Route to Grimentz
Should your plan be to visit Grimentz for overnight accommodation, recross to the western side of the barrage then take a signed footpath (a minor track) winding downhill with footpath shortcuts. In 20mins one of the shortcuts brings you to a sign giving 1hr 30mins to

Below the Moiry barrage, walkers follow the path down to Grimentz

Grimentz. From here the path contours along the hillside among alpenrose, juniper and alder scrub; later with some rock-hopping. In 40mins come to another junction and descend steeply to the road. Cross to the continuing path through rough pasture, then wander downstream along either bank of the stream.

The right bank footpath eventually recrosses the stream and comes onto the road again. Walk ahead a short distance to a bus stop, where you rejoin the path which slopes below the road and shortly gives a good view down to Grimentz and the lower valley. The way loops downhill, crosses to the right side of the stream and follows a track which soon enters forest. In 1hr 30mins at a junction, cross the stream once more onto a tarmac road (camping on the left), and wander down to

> **GRIMENTZ** (1572m, 7hrs) Accommodation, refreshments, shops, bank, PTT, postbus (to Zinal, St Luc, Vissoie, Sierre, etc). Anniviers Tourisme – Bureau de Grimentz, 3961 Grimentz (Tel 027 476 1700, **www.grimentz.ch**). Lower-priced hotels: Le Mélèze, 20 beds (Tel 027 475 12 87, **www. Lemeleze.ch**); Hotel de Moiry, 34 beds (Tel 027 475 11 44, **www.hotel-grimentz.ch**).

There are four optional onward routes from Grimentz:

1 take the **postbus** back to the Barrage de Moiry and follow **Stage 10** to Zinal;

2 follow the **waymarked route** from Grimentz to **Zinal** (2½hrs) where you rejoin the main Chamonix to Zermatt walk at the start of Stage 11;

3 take a **signed route** on footpaths and tracks to **Mission** (30 mins) and then steeply uphill to **Hotel Weisshorn** (described at the end of Alternative Stage 11) in about 4hrs from Grimentz;

4 take the **postbus to St-Luc**, then ride the Tignousa funicular to its top station, and walk (30mins) to **Cabane Bella Tola** (see end of Alternative Stage 11).

STAGE 10

*Cabane de Moiry –
Col de Sorebois – Zinal*

Start	Cabane de Moiry (2825m)
Distance	14km
Height gain	462m
Height loss	1612m
Time	5–5½hrs
High point	Col de Sorebois (2847m)
Map(s)	LS 5028T Monte Rosa–Matterhorn 1:50,000
	or LS 283T Arolla & 273T Montana 1:50,000
Transport options	Postbus (Barrage de Moiry–Grimentz–Zinal)
	Cable-car (Sorebois–Zinal)
Accommodation	Cabane de Sorebois (3¾hrs) – dortoir
	Zinal – hotels, dortoirs

This stage, leading from the arctic splendour of the upper Val de Moiry to the deep forested trench of Val de Zinal (the upper reaches of Val d'Anniviers), entails the crossing of yet another high ridge. This time, however, the effort required to reach it is not unduly fatiguing, while the panorama that greets you on arrival at Col de Sorebois is truly memorable, with Weisshorn and Zinalrothorn on show almost all the way down to Zinal.

After descending along the moraine wall below Cabane de Moiry, a superb belvedere trail carries the route along the hillside heading north about 300m above Lac de Moiry. The hillside is noted for its alpine flowers, and there's also a good chance of catching sight of chamois or even ibex. When the contouring path meets a track above the barrage, our route breaks off to the right and climbs easily to Col de Sorebois. But the toughest part of the day is reserved for the final descent into Zinal – an extremely steep forest path that will aggravate tired knees.

Descend from the hut on the same path used for the approach, and after about 45mins, when you've left the moraine bank and the path becomes wider and easier at an altitude of about 2480m, a path breaks to the right signed to Barrage de Moiry, Col de Sorebois, Zinal. This path, which forms part of the Haut Tour du Lac, follows a fairly regular contour across the grassy hillside. After about 15mins come to a junction where the left-hand option descends to the roadhead car park; the way to Col de Sorebois continues ahead.

It's a very fine path offering splendid views of the glacial landscape you've left behind, and after a while overlooks the jade-green waters of Lac de Moiry and the valley falling away in the distance. Towards the end of the lake the path slopes downhill to meet a grass track at 2385m (2hrs 15mins). Bear right (the lower route descends to the Barrage de Moiry), and begin rising in long loops. When the track makes a long sweep to the

STAGE 10: CABANE DE MOIRY – ZINAL
ALTERNATIVE STAGE 10: BARRAGE DE MOIRY – ZINAL

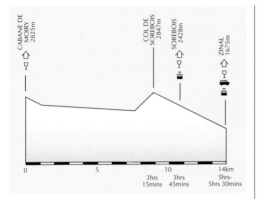

right, a red–white waymark directs you onto a narrow path heading up the grass slope. This takes you all the way to the col – sometimes quite steeply. Views are mostly down-valley towards Grimentz, and there's a possibility of catching sight of chamois and marmots on the way to the pass.

Come onto the saddle of **COL DE SOREBOIS** (2847m, 3hrs 15mins) to be greeted by an incredible panorama of high peaks opposite, dominated by the Weisshorn. Ignore if you can the reshaped ski terrain below and enjoy one of the finest views so far. Though hard to believe, it's a view that improves as you descend.

WEISSHORN

A beautiful mountain with three faces and three ridges, the Weisshorn (4505m) ranks as one of the highest in the Pennine Alps (the second highest standing solely in Switzerland). Forming part of that great ridge which separates Val de Zinal from the Mattertal, the Weisshorn is eye-catching from many different angles, and by the time you reach Zermatt you will have grown very familiar with it. As a mountaineer's mountain the main interest lies in its ridges, and it was by way of the East Ridge that it received its first ascent on 19 August 1861 by the pioneering Victorian scientist and mountaineer John Tyndall (1820–93), with JJ Bennen and Ulrich Wenger as his guides.

Descending to Zinal the trail crosses a pasture near Sorebois, with a panoramic backdrop of iconic snowpeaks

For the descent into Val de Zinal, take a path directly ahead which contours briefly, then angles slightly downhill to join a broader grass path/track beneath a chairlift and continues onto a waymarked piste (5mins from the col). Follow this as it winds down the badly scarred hillside to the cable-car station of

SOREBOIS (2438m, 3hrs 45mins) 35 dortoir places, open mid-June to end of September (Tel 027 475 13 78), refreshments, cable-car to Zinal.

VAL DE ZINAL

The name given to the upper reaches of Val d'Anniviers, Val de Zinal holds much of interest to both walkers and climbers. Indeed, some of the most varied and scenically spectacular walks of the whole Pennine Alps chain are to be enjoyed here, while the big peaks that wall it hold some dramatic routes. The head of the valley is a spectacular amphitheatre of ice and snow with Ober Gabelhorn, Mont Durand, Pointe de Zinal, Dent Blanche, Grand Cornier and the Bouquetins rising from it. Zinalrothorn, Pointe Sud de Moming, Schalihorn and Weisshorn create another cirque in the south-east, while opposite this the pasture bowl of La Lé is backed by another rocky crescent. Evidence of past glaciations can be read quite clearly within the valley itself. For a selection of walks in and around the valley, see *Walking in the Valais*, Kev Reynolds, published by Cicerone Press.

Bear right along a track for 3mins, then take a foot-path branching left signed to Mottec and Zinal. As it winds down the hillside it passes beneath a chairlift and the cableway, then forks. Take the right branch and soon enter forest where the path becomes much steeper and seemingly endless – a knee-jarring descent. ▶ The path is clear and obvious, and a few minutes before reaching the foot of the slope a handrail, followed by a wooden walkway and a footbridge, takes you across a stream flowing down a gully. Keep ahead at a junction 3mins later. There's another footbridge to cross before you come to the Navisence and over this walk up into

Col de Sorebois

An alternative descent on a signed track that passes through La Latta takes a similar time and is easier on the knees.

ZINAL (1675M, 5–5½HRS)

This long-time mountaineering centre is steadily growing at its northern end. The original village, crowded with timber houses and granaries, forms an attractive line along the true right bank of the valley. Zinal is the final settlement in the long Val d'Anniviers; beyond it the valley grows increasingly wild and austere with glaciers, moraine banks and a glorious array of high mountains. Although the majority of walks here entail some pretty steep ascents and descents, Zinal makes an excellent base for a walking or climbing holiday.

Accommodation, ATM, restaurants, shops, supermarkets, PTT, postbus (Zinal–Vissoie–St Luc–Sierre), Bureau des Guides. Office du Tourisme, 3961 Zinal (Tel

027 476 17 05, **www.zinal.ch**). Lower-priced accommodation: Hotel Le Trift, 34 beds (Tel 027 475 14 66, **www.letriftzinal.com**); Auberge Alpina, dortoir & rooms, open mid-June to mid-October (Tel 027 475 12 24, **www.auberge-alpina.ch**); Hotel La Poste, 18 beds (Tel 027 475 11 87, **www.lapostezinal.ch**). Note: The proprietor at Auberge Alpina also has two chalets with kitchen facilities for rent. Telephone number as above.

ALTERNATIVE STAGE 10
Barrage de Moiry –
Col de Sorebois – Zinal

Start	Barrage de Moiry (2249m)
Distance	8km
Height gain	598m
Height loss	1172m
Time	4–4½hrs
High point	Col de Sorebois (2847m)
Map(s)	LS 5028T Monte Rosa–Matterhorn 1:50,000
	or LS 283T Arolla & 273T Montana 1:50,000
Transport options	Postbus (Barrage de Moiry–Grimentz–Zinal)
	Cable-car (Sorebois–Zinal)
Accommodation	Cabane de Sorebois (2½hrs) – dortoir
	Zinal – hotels, dortoirs
Alternative routes	Barrage de Moiry to Zinal or Hotel Weisshorn via
	Grimentz – see details at end of Alternative Stage 9

An easy and straightforward crossing of Col de Sorebois takes the C–Z trekker into the lovely Val de Zinal among the highest mountains of the route since leaving the Mont Blanc massif. On the ascent to the pass there's a distinct possibility of seeing chamois and marmots, while the view from the col itself is awe-inspiring.

From the dortoir just above the Barrage de Moiry wander up the track to the junction with the route of the Haut Tour du Lac which forks right. Ignore this option and continue uphill in long loops for another 20mins, when your track makes a long sweep to the right. Now leave the track for a narrow red–white waymarked path rising up the grass slope on the left. This leads eventually to Col de Sorebois, on occasion with steep zig-zags and long views downvalley towards Grimentz.

You should gain the easy saddle of **COL DE SOREBOIS** (2847m) after about 1hr 40mins to enjoy a magnificent panorama of high peaks dominated by the Weisshorn, that hopefully greets you on arrival.

For the descent to Zinal, which passes the **SOREBOIS** cable-car station (2438m, 2hrs 45mins, accommodation, refreshments, cable-car to Zinal), please see Stage 10.

On the climb to Col de Sorebois

STAGE 11
Zinal – Forcletta – Gruben

Start	Zinal (1675m)
Distance	14km
Height gain	1199m
Height loss	1052m
Time	5½–6hrs
High point	Forcletta (2874m)
Map(s)	LS 5028T Monte Rosa–Matterhorn 1:50,000
	or LS 283T Arolla, 273T Montana & 274T Visp 1:50,000
Transport options	None
Accommodation	Gruben – hotel (beds & matratzenlager/dortoir) and inn (matratzenlager)

The next valley on the eastbound route is the little-known Turtmanntal, with Gruben (otherwise known as Meiden) being the first German-speaking community of the walk. It's a lovely half-forgotten back-water, for the valley is occupied only in summer. Not long after the cattle have been taken down to farms in lowland Switzerland, Gruben closes up until the following spring.

There are two main ways of reaching the Turtmanntal from Zinal: via the Forcletta as per this stage, and over the Meidpass via Hotel Weisshorn or Cabane Bella Tola as described under Alternative Stages 11 and 11A. Both are fine crossings, but the Forcletta has the edge as it is the more direct and, for walkers with limited time available, makes the trek to Zermatt one day shorter than the Meidpass option. It is a magnificent crossing, despite missing the opportunity of staying overnight in Hotel Weisshorn – a memorable experience and, to many, a highlight of the Walker's Haute Route – or the charming Cabane Bella Tola.

Begin in the centre of Zinal, and walk up a narrow road between Hotel Le Trift and the village church. After passing between apartment blocks, branch left on a track towards an extensive block of apartments. About 3mins from the church this track/broad path delivers you onto a road opposite a major group of apartments where a sign-post directs you up a service road – direction Barneuza Alpage and Hotel Weisshorn. This takes you between buildings, then you veer left towards a parking area, then right on a rising gravel track among larch trees. Go through a tunnel and cross an avalanche defence system.

Once across this the path, which is broad and well trodden, begins to make height, but then forks about 15mins from the start. Take the left branch, cross a stream, then climb by a series of steep zig-zags that take you high above the valley. After about 40mins go through a gate, and shortly after take a right fork to rise across an open grass slope, at the top of which the path forks by a low building (**LIREC**). Turn sharply left and climb again into forest where the gradient eases to a more gently rising traverse, and 1hr from the start you come out of the trees to a minor path junction. Continue ahead over a brief hillside shelf (2173m) with a charming backward view to Pigne de la Lé, Grand Cornier and Dent Blanche, while ahead you gaze across the Rhône valley to the line of the Bernese Alps.

Coming out of woodland, the path now develops into a superb belvedere heading north along the hillside, and in due course you will come to the isolated farm of **BARNEUZA ALPAGE** (2211m, 1hr 45mins). Immediately beyond the alp buildings there's a junction of paths; the trail to take is marked to Hotel Weisshorn – the upper path rising ahead.

Autumn colours the hillside on the trail to the Barneuza alpage

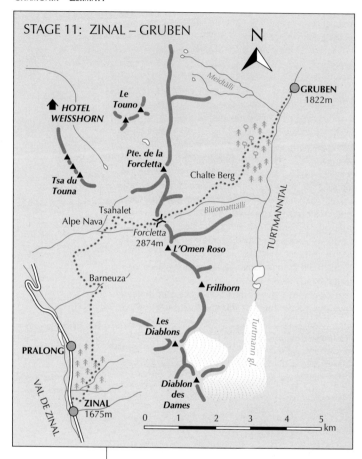

STAGE 11: ZINAL – GRUBEN

GRUBEN
1822m

Meidtälli

Le Touno

HOTEL WEISSHORN

Pte. de la Forcletta

Chalte Berg

Tsa du Touna

Tsahalet

Alpe Nava

Blüomatttälli

Forcletta 2874m

TURTMANNTAL

L'Omen Roso

Barneuza

Frilihorn

PRALONG

Les Diablons

Turtmann gl.

Diablon des Dames

ZINAL
1675m

VAL DE ZINAL

0   1   2   3   4   5 km

About 5mins beyond Barneuza cross a rock tip. Eventually turn a spur and cut into a deep combe whose hillsides are carpeted with juniper, bilberry and alpenrose, and you gain a view ahead towards the Forcletta. Immediately after crossing a stream come to the solitary hut of **ALPE NAVA** (2340m, 2hrs 20mins). A few paces beyond this there's another signed junction. Take the path which climbs to the right (direction Forcletta and Gruben). It rises over grass slopes drained by a stream and is faint in places, but with sufficient red–white way-marks to direct the way.

Skirting the right-hand slope of a bowl of pasture-land enter an upper level, bear left, then rise to the alp of **TSAHALET** (2523m) marked by a large wooden cross. This is gained about 20mins from Alpe Nava.

At the right-hand end of the cattle sheds waymarks direct the continuing path across a rucked and pitted grassland, on the far side of which a clear path takes you up rocky slopes. The way climbs easily in long zig-zags to gain the **FORCLETTA** (2874m, 3hrs 45mins), a bare sad-dle in a ridge stubbed with individual peaklets. Ahead lies the glen of Blüomatttalli, which appears stony and barren – although as you descend through it, you will discover it is full of alpine plants. Looking back from the pass, long distant views include the Aiguilles Rouges above Arolla.

Slant left across a slope of shale, then ease down the left-hand side of the shallow Blüomatttalli where a stream drains between great cushions of moss and flowering plants. Towards the lower end of the glen

The Barneuza alpage, passed on the way to Alpe Nava

the Brunegghorn comes into view to the right across the Turtmanntal, then its long glacier with the Bishorn looking huge to the right of that, and the graceful north ridge of the Weisshorn rising above the Bishorn. "I doubt whether there is a more spiky panorama to be seen in the Alps than this view across the Turtmanntal from the Forcletta descent," wrote Showell Styles in *Backpacking in the Alps and Pyrenees*.

THE TURTMANNTAL

The Turtmanntal is one of the shortest valleys in the Pennine Alps, and one of the least developed. Access from the Rhône valley is by a steeply twisting road via Oberems, but unusually for Switzerland there is no postbus service above that village. The valley itself rises in the south, where the combined ridges of Brunegghorn, Bishorn and Tête de Milon form a lofty wall that never drops below 3500m. (The Weisshorn rises above and to the south of Bishorn and Tête de Milon.)

Both the Turtmann and Brunegg glaciers sweep down from this wall and weld together beneath Les Diablons. Below this junction, on the right bank of the glacier, stands the Turtmann Hut (2520m, 74 places, 3hrs from Gruben), base for climbs on such peaks as the Tête de Milon, Bishorn, Brunegghorn and Barrhorn, the last of these having a tremendous view of the Mattertal and the Mischabel peaks opposite. The valley is completely pastoral, with a number of farms and small hamlets. Cattle graze the lower pastures; sheep roam higher on the hillsides.

Yet again the graceful **Weisshorn** announces its looming presence. In his classic book *The Playground of Europe* Leslie Stephen wrote of the view from just outside Gruben: 'Above us rose the Weisshorn in one of the most sublime aspects of that almost faultless mountain. The Turtmann glacier, broad and white with deep regular crevasses, formed a noble approach, like the staircase of some superb palace. Above this rose the huge mass of the mountain, firm and solid as though its architect wished to eclipse the Pyramids. And, higher still, its lofty crest, jagged and apparently swaying from side to side, seemed to be tossed into the blue atmosphere far above the reach of mortal man. Nowhere have I seen a more delicate combination of mountain massiveness, with soaring and delicately carved pinnacles pushed to the verge of extravagence. Yet few people know of this side of a peak, which every one has admired from the Riffel [above Zermatt].'

The path now veers left over rolling pastures and slopes down to the farm buildings of **CHALTE BERG** (2488m, 4hrs 15mins). Views of the Bishorn, Weisshorn and the snow crest leading to the Tête de Milon are tremendous from here.

The Weisshorn, seen from Chalte Berg on the descent to the Turtmanntal

The mountains at the head of the Turtmanntal

Pass between the alp buildings, where the route is guided by waymarks, directly down the grass slope beyond the alp to an unmade farm road. Turn left along it, and after about 150m bear right on a footpath which descends a little, then runs parallel to the road, later dropping well below it to more alp huts (**MASSSTAFEL** 2235m). When the path brings you onto the road once more, turn right along it for a short distance, then find the continuing path on the right, directly opposite the last hut. This soon brings you onto the road yet again.

There are two routes down to Gruben:

1   starting at a hairpin bend just above where you come onto the road, this option makes a **long traverse** across the hillside to Mittel Stafel where it joins the route from Meidpass (Alternative Stage 11A) to descend to Gruben. On this route watch out for the path signing. If you miss it, a long struggle in a wood lies ahead;

2   the **shorter, recommended option** described here crosses the road and turns right to descend below it.

Cross the road onto the path, which descends below it and soon enters forest where the way zig-zags down. At times the undergrowth beside the path crowds the way, although there's nothing difficult about the descent. This finally brings you to the valley bed by more farm buildings about 1km above Gruben.

Walk towards the valley road, but do not cross the Turtmänna river. Instead take a faint grass path on the left bank and follow this downstream towards Gruben, eventually coming to a path junction near two chalets. Turn right, cross the river and enter

GRUBEN (1822M, 5½–6HRS)

Also known as Meiden, this small village ("more like a Swiss village of the Golden Age of Mountaineering than any other" according to Showell Styles) is the only one in the valley proper – Oberems and Unterems are at the entrance. It consists of a neat cluster of chalets, trim white chapel and hotel above flood-level on the right bank of the Turtmänna stream, idyllically placed between the Meidpass and Augstbordpass by which you leave the valley on the Walker's Haute Route. The small store near Hotel Schwarzhorn stocks a surprising variety of goods. About 500m downvalley from the main village stands the rustic Restaurant Waldesruh. For a time it served as a children's home, then was converted to a youth hostel. It is now a licensed restaurant with matratzenlager accommodation on the second floor.

Accommodation, refreshments, shop. Hotel Schwarzhorn, beds & matratzenlager, open June to October (Tel 027 932 14 14, **www.hotelschwarzhorn.ch**); Restaurant Waldesruh (5mins downvalley), matratzenlager, open mid-June to mid-September (Tel 079 274 62 18).

ALTERNATIVE STAGE 11A
Zinal – Hotel Weisshorn/Cabane Bella Tola

Start	Zinal (1675m)
Distance	10km (14.5km to Cabane Bella Tola)
Height gain	725m (or 892m)
Height loss	63m (or 221m)
Time	3½–4hrs (or 5–5½hrs)
High point	Montagne de Nava, 2400m
Map(s)	LS 5028T Monte Rosa–Matterhorn 1:50,000
	or LS 283T Arolla & 273T Montana 1:50,000
Transport options	Postbus (Zinal to St-Luc), then funicular to Tignousa
Accommodation	Hotel Weisshorn (3½–4hrs)
	Cabane Bella Tola – mountain refuge

The path which runs along a hillside shelf high on the east wall of Val d'Anniviers between Zinal and Hotel Weisshorn provides one of the great walks of Switzerland, and presents such stunning views to the head of the valley that you will probably wish it were possible to walk backwards! The magic of the upper Val d'Anniviers (Val de Zinal), with its crowded mass of snow and ice giants, makes this an alpine wonderland. In order to absorb as much of that magic as possible the day's walk will inevitably take a lot longer than the basic four hours quoted above.

As for Hotel Weisshorn, this large Victorian building lost some of its former eccentricity when it was refurbished a few years ago, but the charm remains, as does the surprise of its setting. A night spent there is counted among the highlights of the Chamonix to Zermatt walk by a large number of trekkers. Advanced booking is recommended – see details at the end of this section.

However, there is an optional extension to Cabane Bella Tola, a privately owned refuge set on pastureland with even better views than those from Hotel Weisshorn. With good facilities, a magical setting and a very fine route to the Meidpass and Gruben next day, this is an option well worth considering.

Follow directions given in Stage 11 (Zinal–Forcletta–Gruben) as far as **ALPE NAVA** (2340m, 2hrs 20mins). Ignore the minor path breaking off to the right (to the Forcletta) and continue ahead (the sign here gives 1hr to Hotel Weisshorn), curving round the combe of Montagne de Nava, crossing a few more streams and rising steadily. In early summer the slopes are lavish with alpine flowers. The southern panorama grows even more impressive and includes the Zinalrothorn, the upper chisel-shaped summit of the Matterhorn and Dent Blanche, and it's worth having plenty of halts to enjoy these views.

We were on course for setting a record for the slowest-ever walk from Zinal to Hotel Weisshorn. Our day had become like Morse code, a succession of dots and dashes as we stumbled along the path among autumn-tinged bilberry leaves now blazing scarlet. Progress was painfully slow, for we had to keep turning to where the southern horizon was an upthrust of spires and domes, a patchwork of grey rock and unmarked snow, of gleaming ice and deep blue shadow. Down below the valley had been brushed with early frost that sparkled as it turned to moisture. Now vegetation had dried in the sunlight, and dark swathes of forest lapped against the lower hillside. Bare grass textured the upper levels with velvet. Then rock, snow and ice appeared far off. The head of the valley was the birthplace of glaciers, and all down Val d'Anniviers we could see a tribute to their industry. It was all too good to ignore, and there could be no haste to this day.

All this route between Zinal and Hotel Weisshorn is used in a mountain marathon that takes place each summer. The yellow-painted letter Z, which appears at many junctions, is a route guide for this race.

Every summer a **mountain marathon** takes place between Sierre in the Rhône valley and Zinal. Not only is it the full marathon distance of over 26 miles (42km), but the amount of height gain is impressive too. Sierre lies at around 550m above sea level, while sections of the path between Hotel Weisshorn and Zinal are at more than 2400m.

About 10mins from Alpe Nava, at the **BELLA LÉ** junction (2400m), another path cuts to the right to the Forcletta; another descends to Ayer, but we continue straight ahead. Rising still, you come onto a gravel track, but leave it a few paces later for a footpath running parallel with it, but at a higher level. On coming to a second track walk along it for about 200m, during which it becomes obvious that this forms part of an avalanche defence system. After 200m leave the track for a footpath rising above it.

The fabulous Val de Zinal headwall, seen from the trail to Hotel Weisshorn

The trail rises and falls across an undulating hillside and soon brings you in sight of Hotel Weisshorn, while an interesting mountain basin is seen off to the right. Shortly after this the path is safeguarded with a fixed chain handrail. You then dip into and through rocky grooves and gullies, then up a rib flanked by bilberries and onto a broad track, where you bear left to reach

HOTEL WEISSHORN (2337m, 3½–4hrs) 37 beds (half-board only), restaurant service – open June to mid-October. Contact: Hotel Weisshorn, 3961 St Luc (Tel 027 475 11 06, **www.weisshorn.ch**) – reservation recommended, particularly over weekends when you should book well ahead.

The large, imposing building of **Hotel Weisshorn** dates from 1882, and has become something of an institution. Set in a magnificent position more than 1000m above the valley bed, it has the Rhône valley to the north, with the chain of the Bernese Alps rising above that. Sunset views are especially fine. The hotel is open from June to mid-October, and from Christmas to mid-April, and is popular for wedding parties and other celebrations.

Continuing Route to Cabane Bella Tola

Walk past Hotel Weisshorn and take a red–white way-marked path ahead, from which you look down onto St-Luc. When the path forks 2mins later take the lower option, shortly after which you curve round the edge of a rocky bluff and continue across bilberry and juniper slopes with a view through the combe of Montagne du Roua, at the head of which lies the Meidpass.

The way angles down to a grass basin, where you keep ahead at two junctions then go up a slope and onto a track to the farm of **TOÛNO LE CHIESSO** (2201m). Turn left along the track/farm road, and when it forks (21mins from Hotel Weisshorn) keep ahead on the upper branch. About 10mins later a sign for Cabane Bella Tola directs you up a path on the right. This contours just above the track, then forks. Take the upper path, which brings you above the farm of **CHALET BLANC DE ROUA** (2179m).

The view at evening from Cabane Bella Tola

Ignore the sign to Bella Tola, which refers to the peak and not the cabane, and go ahead on a narrow path that brings you onto a grass track with occasional waymarks. Rising gently, this curves round the hillside, and 1hr 15mins from Hotel Weisshorn a waymark on the left sends you up the slope on a path which brings you directly to

CABANE BELLA TOLA (2346m, 5–5½hrs) 92 dortoir places, full meals service (Tel 027 475 15 37, cabane@funiluc.ch)

Owned by the St-Luc/Tignousa funicular company, the **Cabane Bella Tola** is a comfortable refuge with good facilities and magnificent views. From its pastureland setting it looks south towards the head of Val de Zinal. Hotel Weisshorn can be seen in the middle distance, but beyond that Weisshorn, Zinalrothorn, Matterhorn and Dent Blanche rim

Cabane Bella Tola, a cosy hut in a pastureland setting with amazing views

the horizon. Behind the refuge rises the 3025m Bella Tola, claimed by some to be the best viewpoint in the Alps, which is reached from the hut by an easy path in a little under 2½hrs. The route to the Meidpass on Alternative Stage 11B passes directly beneath it.

ALTERNATIVE STAGE 11B

Hotel Weisshorn/Cabane Bella Tola –
Meidpass – Gruben

Start	Hotel Weisshorn/Cabane Bella Tola (2337m/2346m)
Distance	9km (10km from Cabane Bella Tola)
Height gain	589m (444m)
Height loss	1104m (968m)
Time	4hrs (or 3½hrs)
High point	Meidpass (2790m)
Map(s)	LS 5028T Monte Rosa–Matterhorn 1:50,000
	or LS 283T Arolla, 273T Montana & 274T Visp 1:50,000
Transport options	None
Accommodation	Gruben – hotel (beds & matratzenlager/dortoir) and inn (matratzenlager)
Alternative route	To Gruben via the Forcletta (see brief note below)

This undemanding day's walk leads out of French-speaking Valais and into German-speaking Wallis – the same canton but linguistically a world apart from that you've been walking through since crossing the Col de Balme.

And it's not just the language that changes either, for a different set of landscapes are in view. On leaving Hotel Weisshorn the way leads through a curiously contorted country en route to the Meidpass (or Meiden Pass as it is also known), while the way down to the Turtmanntal is a descent into the past. The Turtmanntal seems not to belong to the present century – there is a motor road, it is true, and both the Hotel Schwarzhorn and Restaurant Waldesruh have all modern amenities, yet a profound sense of peace prevails, and the valley appears to remain untouched by pressures from the 'outside world'. It is only occupied for part of the year.

The Meidpass route is both direct and interesting, with wonderful views from the actual pass. Whether you begin at Hotel Weisshorn or Cabane Bella Tola, the approach to the pass (the two routes combine 30mins below it) will be inspiring, yet both could challenge your route-finding skills in misty conditions, as there are sections without a visible path. Waymarks or cairns will be your guide.

Out of the hotel turn left where a sign gives 2hrs to the Meidpass. Cross a broad track onto a path (waymarked red–white) from which you look onto St-Luc. When the path forks in 2mins take the lower option, then curve round the edge of a rocky bluff to gain a view ahead through the combe of Montagne de Roua to the Meidpass. The path angles downhill into a grass basin where you go ahead at two junctions, walk up a slope and continue on a track to the farm of **TOÛNO LE CHIESSO** (2201m, 20mins).

Take the minor track that goes up the right-hand side of the farm, takes you between buildings then curves right to climb the slope above the farm, with craggy shapes appearing in the skyline ahead. The track forks 12mins above the farm, where you veer right to approach the solitary building of **LA ROJA** (2308m), which stands within a walled enclosure. A path skirts this and brings you to a signpost. Bear left and wind up the slope through rough pastures mattressed with juniper, alpenrose and bilberry.

Crossing and recrossing streams, pass a tiny pool, from where spiky fingers of rock are seen on the ridge above, and there are distant views of the Bernese Alps to the north. In 55mins there's a signed junction where the right-hand path offers a 5min diversion (plus 5mins back) along a contouring path to visit Lac de Combavert, lying at the foot of a great scree chute spilling from Le Toûno.

Continue up the slope to enter a broader pastureland. As you progress, the path veers a little to the left (north-eastwards) and rises more steeply to meet a stream where it tumbles from an upper basin, which you reach in 1hr 10mins. Where you cross the stream a blue painted sign on a rock directs a route left to 'Lac' – this goes to Lac de l'Armina. Ignore this and head north-east towards the peak of Corne du Boeuf, below which you should be able to see a path zig-zagging to the saddle of the Meidpass.

The landscape becomes more rocky now, but the path is well defined. A few minutes later it crosses another little stream, keeps company with it, then recrosses to its right-hand side by another junction (1½hrs). The left-hand path is the route from Cabane Bella Tola; you turn right for the Meidpass.

Cabane Bella Tola to the Meidpass

Immediately behind the refuge a sign indicates the route to Lac de la Bella Tola. Walk along this path, which rises easily over pastures, goes beneath a ski lift and in 10mins brings you onto a sort of plateau with a farm track scouring through it. Remain on the path for now, but when you come onto the track near another ski tow, walk along it for about 150m until a waymark sends you ahead along the continuing path.

Rising above the track, turn a rocky corner and enter a lovely basin of pasture with a small reedy tarn in it. Keeping left of the tarn, cross a couple of streams feeding into it, then go over more pastures to regain the track. Turn left, and 10mins later bear right while the path to climb Bella Tola goes straight ahead. In another 2mins the track forks; take the right branch and come to the little **LAC DE LA BELLA TOLA** (50mins).

Immediately after crossing the lake's outflow stream the track forks again. Bear right, and very shortly after take a waymarked path on the left to rise over a rocky slope with a few cairns and waymarks to guide you as you cross a spur of rock and grass. After passing beneath another ski tow the path curves left and you gain a first view of the Meidpass; below can be seen **LAC DE L'ARMINA** (2562m).

Descend a little to pass along the north-east side of the lake, and at its far side the path curves left to climb a grass slope, where it is joined by a second path (blue–white waymarks) coming from St-Luc. The route is now waymarked both red–white and blue–white as you climb the slope, and is mostly easy to follow, but in misty conditions concentration will be needed.

Rising eastward make towards the south side of Corne du Boeuf before curving to the right when the slope levels out. You then descend a little, cross two brief rock tips and, 15mins from Lac de l'Armina, come to a signed junction below the Meidpass, where you join the path from Hotel Weisshorn (1½–1¾hrs).

With a few twists the path takes you up into a very stony hollow, goes up its left-hand side, negotiates a scree and rock slope above it, then takes long and gently angled zig-zags across the final approach to the **MEIDPASS** (2790m, 2hrs) – a narrow stony saddle slung between Corne du Boeuf (Meidspitz) to the north and the tower of Pigne de Combavert to the south.

Trail junction below the Meidpass, where the routes from Hotel Weisshorn and Cabane Bella Tola reunite

Just before reaching the pass you gaze back to the distant Mont Blanc de Cheilon, Grand Combin and even Mont Blanc itself. But to the south-east a stony wasteland is buttressed by the lumpy Meidhorn, like the turret of some medieval castle, beyond which gleams the

Weisshorn. Once again this great mountain looks magnificent, the dominant feature in a wild scene of snow-peaks, glaciers and rock.

The path descends easily, albeit a little steeply at first, winding down into the stony basin and keeping to its left-hand side; the basin itself is rimmed with gesticulating fingers of rock with screes spilling below them. Pass to the right of the **MEIDSEE** (2661m), after which the path descends to pastureland with a couple of small tarns in it.

The Meidpass (2790m) is a linguistic border – French to the west, German to the east

There was no wind, no breeze, no sound of streams or falling stones, nor of marmot, sheep or cowbell. We were both so struck by the overpowering sense of peace and stillness that we stopped for a minute and listened. And it was true. It was as though even the Earth itself had ceased to spin; as though all and everything had momentarily been frozen in time. There were no sounds. Before I had always believed that so long as there was life there could be no such thing as silence – there would be some semblance of sound, if only the hum of distance. But this was the nearest I had ever come to total soundlessness. We'd entered a zone of silence.

The path leads to the alp hamlet of **OBER STAFEL** – the 'upper alp' at 2334m where you come onto a track. A few paces along this leave it for a continuing path which descends steeply to the lower alp (**MITTEL STAFEL**), with its view upvalley to the Turtmann glacier, off to the left to the glaciers of Wildstrubel and Balmhorn in the Bernese Alps, and to the cone of the lovely Bietschhorn which rises above the Lötschental on the far side of the unseen Rhône valley.

The impressive and very difficult **Bietschorn** ('whose attractions are so overwhelming that it cannot escape perpetual attraction' – according to RLG Irving) is seen to the north in the line of the Bernese Alps. An isolated mountain of 3934m, it stands high above the tranquil Lötschental, which it dominates by its powerful presence. It was first climbed by Leslie Stephen and his guides on 13 August 1859.

Gruben, overnight base for walkers bound for the Augstbordpass

A narrow path takes you through the hamlet of chalets and barns (water supply), then descends another steep grass slope before angling gently to the left to enter a forest of stone pine and larch. This brings you down to the valley floor. Cross the Turtmänna stream by a bridge and walk up the opposite slope to reach the small village of

GRUBEN (1822m, 4hrs). For details see notes at the end of Stage 11.

STAGE 12
Gruben – Augstbordpass – St Niklaus

Start	Gruben (1822m)
Distance	16km
Height gain	1072m
Height loss	1767m
Time	6½–7hrs
High point	Augstbordpass (2894m)
Map(s)	LS 5028T Monte Rosa–Matterhorn 1:50,000
	or LS 274T Visp 1:50,000
Transport option	Cable-car (Jungen–St Niklaus)
Accommodation	Jungen (5–5½hrs) – matratzenlager
	St Niklaus – hotels, pensions

This stage is one of the finest of them all, and a walk to stand comparison with almost any other day's outing in the Pennine Alps. It has so many contrasts, so many features that capture one's attention. It has history too, for the Augstbordpass which links the Turtmanntal with the Mattertal was used from the Middle Ages onward as an important trading route between the Rhône valley and Italy – a route that originally continued from St Niklaus to Zermatt and over the glacial Theodule Pass beside the Matterhorn.

Crossing the final pass on the Chamonix to Zermatt route is a highlight in every sense of the word. Never as demanding as the total height gain and loss might suggest, it leads through spacious woodland, over high pastures and into a stony wilderness, but then opens to some of the loveliest views in all Switzerland. The Matterhorn does not feature in these views, however, but remains hidden until you are committed to the Europaweg on the far side of the Mattertal. But other high peaks – most notably the Dom (the highest peak entirely within Swiss territory) – add much to the scene, while the Mattertal itself appears as an incredibly deep trench of greenery walled by grey rock and forest another world away.

Then comes the descent into that world, and this too is full of pleasures and the odd surprise – none greater or more beautiful than the discovery of the little hamlet of Jungen clinging to the desperately steep mountain slopes high above St Niklaus. Not an unreal tourist haunt, this is a living, working, daily active alp hamlet, and one of the last such remote farming communities to be met on the Walker's Haute Route.

From Jungen the path plunges once again into forest, dropping into the shadowed depths of the Mattertal past a series of tiny white shrines as views of the valley are rearranged with almost every step.

The way to the Augstbordpass begins on the south side of Hotel Schwarzhorn, where a grassy trail heads straight up the slope towards sparse woods of larch and pine. This soon becomes a generous path with long weaving zigzags on which you gain height without too much effort.

In a little under an hour you will arrive at the four-way path junction of **GRÜOBUALP** (2151m). Ignore alternatives and continue uphill (the right-hand option goes to the Turtmann Hut). Emerging from the woods, about 15mins from the Grüobualp junction, come onto the remains of a dirt road created to service the construction of an avalanche defence system. The hillside has been mostly reinstated now, and you bear right along what appears to be a slightly broader path which soon cuts up to the left and offers a view of the avalanche defences. The continuing climb winds up to an open shelf occupied by the two alp buildings of **OBER GRÜOBU STAFEL** (2369m, 1hr 20mins) with wide views across the valley to the Meidpass.

Passing to the right of the huts the path continues uphill to the left of a stream in the hanging valley

STAGE 12: GRUBEN – ST NIKLAUS

*Rockbound
pool below the
Augstbordpass*

of Grüobtälli. The path later crosses and recrosses this
stream, and there are no unduly steep sections as you
rise to a lumpy inner region with screes lining the southern wall of peaks, and grassy hummocks elsewhere littered with grey-green lichened rocks. As with the basin
below the Meidpass, this area too is a place where few
sounds intrude on a windless day.

After about 2½hrs the trail steepens as you rise over
a rocky step, then descend slightly to skirt a small pond
before curving left and rising again, this time at a steady
incline on the final stretch to the **AUGSTBORDPASS**
(2894m, 3hrs).

The pass overlooks a wild and rock-strewn wilderness, a landscape of austere beauty. Ahead in the
distance rises the pointed, glacier-draped Fletschhorn
(3919m) above the vague hint of the Saastal, while in the
middle distance northern outliers of the great Mischabel
wall, with Balfrin and Ulrichshorn above the Ried glacier, spread in a lavish show of grandeur.

FLETSCHHORN

Rising high above the village of Saas Balen in the Saastal, the Fletschhorn (3993m) is a mountain of some complexity and one which, though little known outside climbing circles, commands a certain respect. Its twisted ridges ensure that every view of it is different. Glaciers sweep down on each side between extended rocky spurs. Immediately to the south is the Lagginhorn, with the Boshorn to the north. The Fletschhorn received its first ascent in 1854.

Given sufficient time, energy and inclination, the Schwarzhorn to the north of the pass would be worth a visit (1hr from the pass by path most of the way). The summit has the reputation of being one of the great viewpoints of the Alps. The panorama is "one of surpassing magnificence": to the north is a memorable spread of the Bernese Alps, including Finsteraarhorn and Doldenhorn; to the south the view takes in Monte Rosa, Liskamm, Weisshorn and Dent Blanche; and to the east the Ticino Alps blaze a blue horizon, while nearer to hand rise the Mischabel chain, Weissmies, Fletschhorn and Monte Leone.

MISCHABEL

Mischabel is the name given to that huge wall of peaks that forms the western section of Saas Fee's noted amphitheatre and makes an effective divide between the Saastal and the Mattertal. The Mischabel wall consists of Täschhorn, Dom and Lenzspitze, with a spur going north-west to include the Nadelhorn. It's a consistently high wall whose crest nowhere falls below 4000m. A bivouac hut stands on the Mischabeljoch at the southern end, while the Mischabel huts (there are two) are perched on a rib of rock between the Hohbalm and smaller Fall glaciers. The western flanks are served by the Täsch, Kin, Dom and Bordier huts. Only the northern outliers of the Mischabel group are seen at first from the Augstbordpass.

A clear path drops in zig-zags to a stony bowl on the eastern side – the cirque that cups the Inners Tälli. Progressing steeply at first, the way eases lower down and, 25mins from the pass, squeezes through a rocky cleft, emerging to scant grass littered with rocks. About 10mins later you come to a junction of paths, taking the right-hand option (signed to Jungen and St Niklaus) that slopes down and then veers over to the right-hand side of the valley after crossing the Emdbach stream.

The route now embarks on a gently rising traverse of the southern flank of the valley, heading east across a slope of boulders and rocks. But it's a well-made path which brings you to a shoulder at 2488m, where you gain a first sighting of the deep cut of the Mattertal. Off to the left can be seen the Grosser Aletschgletscher.

THE MATTERTAL AND THE GROSSER ALETSCHGLETSCHER

The Vispertal strikes south from the Rhône valley for 7km to Stalden, where it forks. To the south-east lies the Saastal, cut by the Saaservispa river, while south-westward runs the Mattertal, the valley of the Mattervispa river. At its head lies Zermatt, with the Matterhorn towering over it. The **Mattertal** is a narrow, deeply cut valley flanked by the highest peaks in Switzerland. The eastern wall is that of the Mischabelhörner (see above); the western wall contains such magnificent peaks as Zinalrothorn, Schalihorn, Weisshorn, Bishorn and Brunegghorn; while the valley is blocked in the south by the glacier-hung mountains that run westward from Monte Rosa – Liskamm, Castor, Pollux, Breithorn and Matterhorn.

Seen to the north as a great ice river on the far side of the Rhône valley, the **Grosser Aletschgletscher** is the longest glacier in the Alps. It flows for some 25km, draining such Oberland peaks as Mittaghorn, Gletscherhorn, Jungfrau, Mönch and Fiescherhorn. Some very fine walks, accessible from Riederalp, Bettmeralp or Kühboden, may be had on footpaths that run alongside the lower reaches of this glacier. (See *Walking in the Valais* by Kev Reynolds, a walking guide also published by Cicerone Press.)

Continuing round the mountainside the path narrows and is exposed in places (**care required**). It climbs one or two rock steps then turns a spur (**TWÄRA** 2500m, 4½hrs),

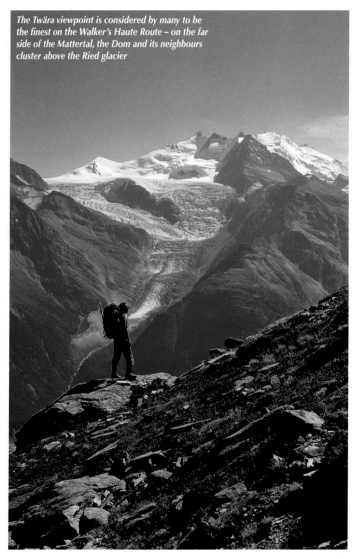

The Twära viewpoint is considered by many to be the finest on the Walker's Haute Route – on the far side of the Mattertal, the Dom and its neighbours cluster above the Ried glacier and there before you is one of those rare sights that is so overwhelmingly powerful that all else is forgotten.

Across the gulf of the Mattertal soar Nadelhorn, Lenzspitze and Dom, with the Ried glacier pouring into the shoe-horn trough it has carved above Grächen's green terrace. It is a stunning vision, full of drama and grace of form, a perfect symbol of mountain architecture. Then, right at the head of the Mattertal, are Liskamm, Castor and Pollux and the long white block of the Breithorn, with the smaller pyramid of the Klein Matterhorn next to it. (The Matterhorn itself remains shyly hidden behind the black outline of the Mettelhorn.)

THE DOM

At 4545m the Dom is the highest individual mountain in Switzerland, since the Dufourspitze on Monte Rosa (4634m) is shared with Italy. The summit tops the Mischabel wall. From it the Festi glacier flows steeply westward, while the Hohberggletscher falls to the north-west and is fed by the neighbouring Lenzspitze and Nadelhorn. The normal ascent route from the Dom Hut follows the right bank of the Festigletscher, crosses the Festijoch and then makes a broad sweep up the head of the Hohberggletscher towards the summit. The Dom was first climbed in 1858, and received an early ski ascent (by Arnold Lunn and Joseph Knubel) in 1917.

This spur of mountainside is surely the crowning glory of the Walker's Haute Route, a route that presents one visual gem after another from start to finish.

A few more paces and, most stunning of all, the Weisshorn yet again announces its domineering presence above and behind the Brunegghorn that rises in one immense shaft nearly 2500m out of the valley. ◄

Beyond the viewpoint the route follows a paved mule-path for a short distance on huge flat slabs, before you descend steeply on a footpath with a view into the Jungtal hanging valley. With numerous twists the path leads down the very steep grass hillside to another junction. Continue ahead towards the first larch trees; 3mins later come to the Unterer Läger junction at 2255m and turn right. At yet another junction by a drystone wall you catch sight of Jungen and follow the trail towards it. Through larchwoods the path splits into several braidings, but these reunite just before you enter the hamlet of

JUNGEN (1955M, 5½HRS)

Perched on a steep slope of mountainside 900m above the Mattertal, with which it is linked by cableway, Jungen is a delightful collection of old timber chalets and haybarns, with a white painted chapel and restaurant, the Junger-Stübli, nearby. In the early summer cheese is made in a building at the western entrance to the hamlet, but when the cattle are moved up into the Jungtal the cheesemaker goes with them. A very fine high route, the Moosalp–Jungen Höhenweg, roughly follows the 2000m contour north-east for about 9km. (**Note** The LS map names this hamlet Jungu.)

Limited 6-place matratzenlager accommodation is available in a local chalet – apply at the Junger-Stübli (Tel 027 956 21 01); refreshments, cable-car to St Niklaus. Note that maps and local signs give Jungen as Jungu.

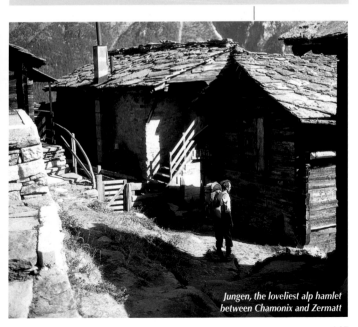

Jungen, the loveliest alp hamlet between Chamonix and Zermatt

As soon as we saw the hamlet from the path way above it, we knew instinctively that it would offer something special, and it did. Coming down to Jungen reinforced that initial instinct. First there was the visual dimension – a quintessential alp hamlet of almost black timbers with a long, dramatic view to the head of the valley. The valley lay 900m below; the Dom (4545m) soared up to full height opposite, a white crust above the rocky Grubenhorn, with the Ried glacier peeling through its funnel; Brunegghorn and Weisshorn above to the right dazzled in the afternoon sunlight. We wandered between the buildings and, just below the chapel, saw a restaurant, the Junger-Stübli, and couldn't resist stopping there for a drink with that view before us. Our original plan had been to continue down to St Niklaus, but when we realized there was a bed to be had here, our plan changed instantly. St Niklaus could wait until tomorrow. That evening we studied the mountains through binoculars, noting the light of the Bordier Hut opposite below the Balfrin, and another at the head of the valley where a glow-worm sized train moved slowly against the black mountain shapes towards the Gornergrat – a world remote from ours. Jungen was full of magic and we spent a memorable night there, enjoying first-class hospitality (that has been repeated on every return since) in a setting that is nothing short of pure enchantment.

The path through Jungen leads to the chapel (if you prefer to descend by cable-car turn left at an obvious junction in the middle of the hamlet on a path that goes directly to the cableway station). From the chapel descend steeply below the restaurant and wind in zig-zags into forest. Beside the forest path you will pass a whole series of small white shrines, most of which have been dedicated by Mattertal families.

About 35mins below Jungen there's a footpath junction where you continue straight ahead – the alternative trail cuts sharply back to the left. Cross a rocky cleft on a footbridge over the Jungbach stream, beyond which the gradient is less severe. The way winds on, still through forest as it works round the lower hillside, then between small parcels of meadowland to reach the railway station at

ST NIKLAUS (1127M, 6½–7HRS)

This is the main village of the valley, formerly known as Gassen. St Niklaus has a 17th-century church with an onion-domed spire similar to many seen in the Tyrol. Home to a number of well-known guiding families of the Golden Age and post-Golden Age of Mountaineering, including the Knubels and Pollingers, the village has a mountain guides museum, the *Bergführer, Heimat- und Mineralienmuseum* (open Tues & Fri, 16.00–18.00, from mid-July to end of September).

Accommodation, refreshments, shops, banks, PTT, railway (to Zermatt and Visp), cable-car to Jungen, bus to Grächen and Gasenried. Tourismusbüro, 3924 St Niklaus (Tel 027 956 36 63, **www.st-niklaus.ch**). Lower priced accommodation: Hotel La Réserve (Tel 027 955 22 55, **www.la-reserve.ch**); Pension Walliserkeller (Tel 027 956 11 60, **www.walliserkeller.ch**); Pension Edelweiss (Tel 027 956 26 16).

Before deciding on overnight accommodation in St Niklaus consider your onward plan. Should you decide to opt for the high route to Zermatt via the Europaweg (Stages 13 & 14) you may choose to take the bus to Gasenried (saving an uphill walk of 1½–2hrs) in order to tackle the first stage of the Europaweg tomorrow. In this case the bus leaves from just outside St Niklaus railway station. (For accommodation in Gasenried see Stage 12A.) However, should your plan be to walk the original valley route to Zermatt, your best bet is to overnight in St Niklaus. Before committing yourself to the Europaweg, you are strongly advised to read the warning notes in the introduction to Stage 13.

STAGE 12A
St Niklaus – Gasenried

Start	St Niklaus (1127m)
Distance	4km
Height gain	532m
Time	1½–2hrs
High point	Gasenried (1659m)
Map(s)	LS 5028T Monte Rosa–Matterhorn 1:50,000
	or LS 274T Visp 1:50,000
Transport option	Bus (St Niklaus–Gasenried)
Accommodation	Gasenried – hotel with matratzenlager
Alternative routes	St Niklaus to Grächen (see below)

This very short walk is an important linking stage which brings the Haute Route trekker to the start of the two-day Europaweg leading to Zermatt. As mentioned at the end of the previous stage, an alternative option would be to take the bus from St Niklaus to Gasenried – either on arrival at St Niklaus or early next morning – to enable you to set off fresh for the Europa Hut. Since the first stage of the Europaweg leading to the Europa Hut is quite demanding, it would not be advisable to add this (admittedly short) walk to the beginning. Better to have a comfortable night in Gasenried before setting out. There are some pleasant, scenic local walks above the village to help fill the day.

Since there's only one hotel in Gasenried (modestly priced and with matratzenlager) it is advisable to telephone ahead to ensure there are beds available. Should the hotel be fully booked an alternative suggestion is to walk (or bus) to Grächen, where there's plenty of accommodation. An outline of the route to Grächen is given below, and it's an easy 30min walk from there to Gasenried for the continuing Europaweg.

From the village square below St Niklaus railway station walk down an alley to the main street and cross directly ahead into Eyeweg. This leads to a bridge over both the main valley road and the Mattervispa river, which you

STAGE 12A: ST NIKLAUS – GASENRIED

cross and turn left. After passing a number of houses come to the Grächen road. Cross this and walk along a minor road rising among more houses. It curves to the right and reaches a staggered crossroads. Once again cross over and continue ahead. When the road ends on the edge of woodland a footpath takes the onward route over a stream, then climbs among trees. On emerging from the woods this path makes a rising traverse of the steeply sloping hillside overlooking the northern outskirts of St Niklaus.

About 20mins above St Niklaus you come to the collection of old timber chalets of **WICHUL** (1195m) where you bear right onto a narrow road. This curves sharply to the right about 50m later.

Detour to Grächen

The route to Grächen slants left, rising among pinewoods, crosses and recrosses the road on the way to **RITTINEN** (1455m, 1hr 15mins), then continues via **NIEDER-GRÄCHEN** 15min later, where a footpath climbs among chalets and hay-barns to reach the attractive resort of

171

GRÄCHEN (1615M, 2HRS)

Sprawling along a sun-trap of a terrace on the east side of the Mattertal, about 500m above St Niklaus, this very pleasant resort attracts visitors in winter and summer. By judicious use of the Seetalhorn and Hannigalp cableways some tremendous viewpoints are easily accessible, but even without this mechanical aid, numerous footpaths give scenically rewarding walks. There are two classic long walks from here. The first is the **Balfrin Höhenweg** (or Höhenweg Saas Fee as it's also known), which makes a challenging high-level route to Saas Fee by a series of former shepherds' paths, and was opened in 1954. This takes 7–7½hrs to complete. The other long route is the 31km **Europaweg** (opened July 1997) between Grächen and Zermatt, which now forms the last two stages of the Chamonix to Zermatt Walker's Haute Route. With plenty of accommodation choices, Grächen makes a good base for a walking holiday.

Accommodation, restaurants, shops, banks, PTT, bus (St Niklaus–Grächen). Tourismusbüro (tourist office), 3925 Grächen (Tel 027 955 60 60, www. graechen.ch). Lower priced accommodation: Hotel Alpha (b&b rates plus self-catering facilities, www.alpha-graechen.ch) (Tel 027 956 13 01); Hotel Alpina, 10% discount for Europaweg walkers – password: "Europaweg-Wanderer Tour Monte-Rosa" (Tel 027 955 26 00, www.hotelalpinagraechen.ch); Hotel Garni Abendruh (Tel 027 956 11 16); Hotel Sonne (Tel 027 956 11 07); Hotel Pension Bellevue (Tel 027 956 33 30, www.bellevue-graechen.ch).

The onward route to Gasenried begins by the parish church on Dorfplatz and is well signed. It is part of the Europaweg and takes an easy 30mins to join Stage 13.

Keep to the road for a few more paces after the sharp right bend, then go sharply left then right on a narrow footpath climbing along the edge of a meadow to emerge onto the St Niklaus–Grächen road. Turn left, and almost immediately break to the right on the continuing footpath rising among woods of larch and pine.

Climbing in fairly steep zig-zags through forest, the way emerges onto the road again. Bear right and turn the hairpin bend, from which you gain a tremendous view upvalley. About 100m after the hairpin cut back to the right on a track rising among trees. When it forks soon after by a timber building take the upper route.

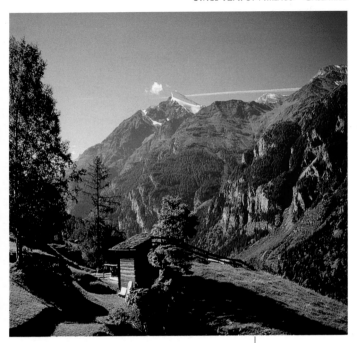

The short climb to Gasenried is a visual delight for much of the way

This winds uphill, and on reaching a four-way path junction (1hr from St Niklaus) you continue ahead. The next junction is met by a shrine and a crucifix, where you bear right to make a final climb to Gasenried, soon passing between vegetable plots with the village seen above.

The lower part of the village is reached in about 1hr 20mins, and from here you gain views north to the Bernese Alps, with the pointed Bietschhorn prominent in that view. Follow a narrow road which rises steeply to the main part of Gasenried where the Ried glacier is seen at the head of a hanging valley behind the village. The only hotel, the Alpenrösli, is situated in the square near the church.

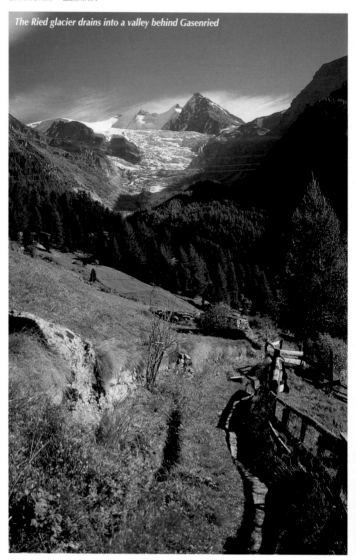

The Ried glacier drains into a valley behind Gasenried

*Gasenried at the start
of the Europaweg*

GASENRIED (1659M, 1HR 40MINS)

This low-key neighbour of Grächen's is dug into the steep hillside a little further south. The village stands on two levels and consists of a number of typical Valaisian chalets and granaries, while just above it footpaths cut through steep pastures and forests to extend the views. The valley of the Riedbach torrent lies behind Gasenried, with the Ried glacier hanging in its upper reaches. As a holiday base, Gasenried would suit any walkers not interested in 'night life'. It's a quiet place with lots of opportunities for walkers.

Accommodation, restaurants, shop, PTT, bus (St Niklaus–Gasenried). Tourismusbüro, 3924 St Niklaus (Tel 027 956 36 63). Hotel Alpenrösli, 28 beds, 10 matratzenlager places; open June–October (Tel 027 956 17 81).

STAGE 13
Gasenried – Europa Hut

Start	Gasenried (1659m)
Distance	14km
Height gain	1131m
Height loss	570m
Time	5½–6½hrs
High point	North of Galenberg (2690m)
Map(s)	LS 5028T Monte Rosa–Matterhorn 1:50,000
	or LS 274T Visp & 284T Mischabel 1:50,000
Transport options	None
Accommodation	Europa Hut – mountain refuge
Alternative route	St Niklaus to Zermatt via the Mattertal – see Alternative Stage 13
Note	The nature of this stage makes timing really quite variable. Strong parties will find these times generous, while less-strong parties may need considerable extra time.

Created in 1997, the Europaweg is a challenging route stretching 31km between Grächen and Zermatt, which climbs high above the Mattertal – as much as 1400m above the valley in some places – with one tremendous viewpoint after another to make it a visual extravaganza virtually from start to finish. One of the best panoramas is enjoyed about two hours after setting out, when the Matterhorn at last reveals itself at the head of the valley. The Bietschhorn is seen in the other direction, Dom and Ried glacier to the south-east, and Weisshorn to the south-west, plus numerous other peaks, each of which would be a major attraction in any other range (www.europaweg.ch).

Warning It will take a total of 11–12hrs to walk these two stages from Gasenried to Zermatt, and by far the majority of the Europaweg is as safe as can be expected. This is a high mountain path, different in character from much of the Walker's Haute Route. The walker is subjected to almost constant exposure and if you don't deal with this well or are less than totally surefooted, you are strongly advised not to attempt the route. There are several places (the first about 2½hrs from Gasenried) that are potentially dangerous from stonefall or other objective hazards where walkers are urged to be extra vigilant and to move quickly over the danger areas.

There are countless sections safeguarded with lengths of fixed rope, too. The Europaweg, which is publicised as part of the misnamed Swiss Tour of Monte Rosa and also forms a section of the Tour of the Matterhorn, has become extremely popular, but everyone who tackles it should make his or her own judgement whether the risks outlined here (and marked with warning signs on the trail itself) are worth taking. Should you think not, then follow the one-day valley route described as Alternative Stage 13.

The unstable nature of the Europaweg cannot be overstated. Of all stages of the Walker's Haute Route, the route of the Europaweg is particularly vulnerable to change; heavy rains, snowmelt, frost and the general instability of the mountain environment can all have an effect, and it is likely that some sections described here will be different by the time you come to tackle them. Where the path is different from that described, please follow Europaweg signs which should indicate the current route. The website www.europaweg.ch gives frequent updates as to the state of the route and any major diversions in place, and the warden at the Europa Hut is well-placed to advise on day-by-day conditions.

The Europaweg remains a tough, challenging but rewarding finale to the Walker's Haute Route, but all who tackle it should only do so after careful consideration of the risks involved. Before setting out, you are strongly advised to telephone ahead to the Europa Hut to book bedspace for the night. In the high season it is likely to be very busy.

On the early stage of the Europaweg above Gasenried

STAGE 13: GASENRIED – EUROPA HUT

N

GRÄCHEN
1615m

WICHUL

ST NIKLAUS
1127m

GASENRIED
1659m

Matter Vispa

▲ *Grat*

Grosse
Graben

MATTSAND

▲ *Breithorn*
3178m

Ried glacier

HERBRIGGEN

▲

Europaweg

MATTERTAL

▲ *Dirruhorn*
4035m

Hobarg glacier

▲ *Nadelhorn*
4327m

▲ *Lenzspitze*
4294m

EUROPA HUT
2220m

RANDA

▲ *Dom*
4497m

0   1   2   3   4   5
km

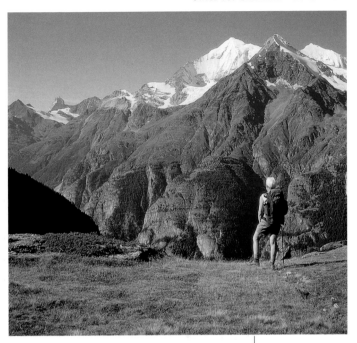

Follow the road past the church in Gasenried curving left into the Riedbach valley. On reaching a small chapel the road forks. Take the lower option, which becomes a track leading past a picnic area to a bridge spanning the Riedbach torrent. Over the bridge immediately turn left on a path which climbs steeply for a few minutes, then, at a poorly marked junction, contours to the right through woodland. Before long the path climbs again, twisting uphill, steeply most of the time, and with the way clearly signed at all junctions.

As you gain height occasional views are glimpsed through the trees to the Bietschhorn in the distance and Gasenried below. In 1hr 50mins reach a viewpoint (**GRAT** 2300m) with a stunning panorama that concentrates on the chain of the Bernese Alps and the gleaming Grosser

Once again the Weisshorn makes its presence felt – this time on the early stage of the Euroweg

This statue of St Bernard stands just above the Grat viewpoint

Aletschgletscher, while through a gap spikey peaks on the west side of the Mattertal will be recognised as being on show on the descent into the Turtmanntal from the Forcletta on Stage 11; the most conspicuous of these is the 3411m Gässispitz. Just above the viewpoint a large cross extends the view and makes a very fine belvedere.

The path now curves through the rocky gap to a view of the Barrhorn and Weisshorn, and 5mins later you gain another wonderful viewpoint at 2335m, marked by a signpost, from where the unmistakable Matterhorn can be seen upvalley. Bear left and climb higher up the ridge, guided by waymarks and cairns, to emerge onto a broad open shoulder on which there's a statue of St Bernard off to the left (2460m, 2hrs 10mins). From this point the Riedgletscher is seen to good effect to the south-east – the Bordier Hut can also be seen from here on the east bank of the glacier.

The statue of **St Bernard** on the viewpoint of the Mittelberg ridge commemorates the opening of the Europaweg in 1997. This patron saint of mountain

Two hours from Gasenried, a viewpoint looks onto the Ried glacier

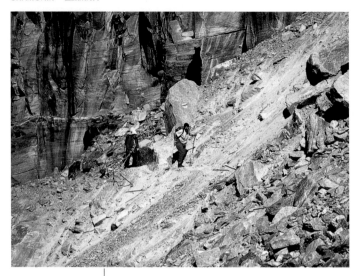

Stonefall danger area in the Grosse Graben combe, 2½ hours from Gasenried

travellers was formerly Archdeacon of Aosta, Bernard of Menthon, who had spent many years caring for travellers and pilgrims in trouble after crossing the alpine pass named after him, and who was responsible for the construction of the original hospice there. Bernard died in the 1080s and was beatified shortly after. In 1923 Pope Pius XI confirmed St Bernard as patron saint of the Alps.

The Europaweg continues to rise, crossing a rocky area to another path junction, where you continue straight ahead. Here the trail has been forced across a very rough slope, and about 2½hrs from Gasenried you reach the first major challenges of boulders, exposed scree and particularly stonefall in the Grosse Graben combe. Much of this combe is in an unstable condition, and in two places signs warn trekkers to cross the danger areas quickly. A combination of caution and speed is advised.

On the south side of the combe beneath the Breithorn there are several fixed rope sections, but on rounding a rocky spur at about 2690m you reach the highest part of the Europaweg and gain yet more stunning views of the Weisshorn. The way then descends a little, before zig-zagging up to pass round another spur and contour to a wooden walkway followed by another fixed rope section (4hrs). At this point the greatest difficulties are behind you. Just beyond this another signpost gives 35mins to Galenberg and 1hr 50mins to the hut (a tough challenge indeed).

> Flanking the Ried glacier the **Breithorn** (3178m) forms part of the long north-west arête running down from the Nadelhorn, and is just one of many mountains in the Swiss Alps to bear this name, which means, literally, 'broad mountain'. Perhaps the best known of the Breithorns is that which carries the Swiss/Italian border above Zermatt. Others of note are the Lauterbrunnen Breithorn and Lötschental Breithorn, and there's another above the Simplon Pass not far from Monte Leone.

Views now include the snowy mass of the Zermatt Breithorn at the head of the valley on the border with Italy. There follows another lengthy fixed rope section, and in 4hrs 45mins you come to the **GALENBERG** junction (2600m) where one path descends to Herbriggen, which lies in the valley midway between St Niklaus and Randa (a 2hr descent). At this junction take the upper path ahead, now with a clear view across the valley to the site of a massive rockfall above Randa. The route contours round a huge and steep valley; after rising a little the path loops down to lose about 250m of height and reaches yet another path junction (5½hrs). The Europa Hut is signed 45mins.

> In April 1991 a massive **rockfall** reshaped the mountainside north-west of Randa when a vast section of the Langenflueberg collapsed into the valley, demolishing the railway, blocking the river and cutting off the upper Mattertal for several days.

No matter how solidly the bridges on the Europaweg are built, they are blown away by the rockfall on this lower slope of the Dom

The way curves into a hillside 'bay' overhung by séracs of the Hobarg glacier. There is some minor danger of falling ice, and for a short stretch there are warning signs by the path. Crossing glacial streams, first on a wooden bridge, then a small bridge (avoiding the stream bed under wet conditions), shortly followed by a 30m suspension bridge over a deep gully (cross with care), the way contours round the south side of the 'bay' and comes to the Miesboden spur (2280m), another splendid viewpoint. From here the path twists down among a few larches to reach the

EUROPA HUT (2220m, 6hrs 20mins) Owned by the Randa gemeinde, staffed from mid-June to mid-October, 42 places, full meals service (Tel 027 967 82 47, **www.europaweg.ch**). The hut is a fine timber-built refuge, opened in 1999, with views directly across the valley to the Weisshorn and upvalley to the Breithorn, Klein Matterhorn, Mettelhorn and Schalihorn.

STAGE 14
Europa Hut – Täschalp – Zermatt

Start	Europa Hut (2220m)
Distance	18km
Height gain	348m
Height loss	962m
Time	6½–7hrs
High point	Sunnegga (2288m)
Map(s)	LS 5028T Monte Rosa–Matterhorn 1:50,000
	or LS 284T Mischabel 1:50,000
Transport options	Sunnegga Express funicular (Sunnegga–Zermatt)
	Bus (Winkelmatten–Zermatt)
Accommodation	Täschalp (Ottavan) (3½hrs) – matratzenlager
	Zermatt – hotels, pensions, matratzenlager, youth hostel, camping

A series of rockfalls beyond the Europa Hut have currently changed the route as described, with a section being closed off and a detour sending walkers down to the valley near Randa. A signed path then climbs steeply back again to rejoin the original trail below the privately-owned Kin Hut (Kinhütte, 2584m, 32 places, Tel 027 967 86 18). This diversion will add about 2hrs to the overall time to reach Zermatt. However, as work is ongoing to restore the trail, and much of the way to Zermatt is unaffected, the original route description remains in the following pages. **Note** Rather than face the steep ascent from Randa, some Haute Route walkers report continuing along the Mattertal to Täsch, then walking (or taking a taxi) up to Täschalp to rejoin the final stage of the trek there.

For up-to-date information about the state of the trail to Zermatt, enquire at the Europa Hut.

On leaving the Europa Hut the path slopes downhill and 5mins later comes to a junction with the Dom Hut path. Continue to descend, and in another 5mins a second junction (**DOMHÜTTENWEG** 2149m) directs the

STAGE 14: EUROPA HUT – ZERMATT

Europaweg straight ahead, while the alternative path descends to Randa.

The way now slants uphill to hug a band of cliffs, where you duck behind a waterfall. The path descends and soon after is directed steeply upwards to a new suspension bridge. (Two months after it was opened, this 230m bridge was destroyed by rockfall. At the time of writing a replacement continues the route – but be alert for changes.) After the bridge, pass through sparse larchwoods and come to yet another path junction with a second descent option to Randa. On emerging from the woods the Matterhorn comes into view ahead.

THE MATTERHORN

Standing on the borders of Switzerland and Italy like some gigantic frontier post, at 4477m the Matterhorn is the most easily recognised of all Alpine peaks, its distinctive pyramid shape having been adopted as the very symbol of Switzerland. Not unnaturally it is the focus of attention of practically every visitor to Zermatt, and there can be few mountain activists who do not, at some time or another, feel a longing to climb it.

Edward Whymper's obsession has been shared by many in the 140-odd years that have passed since his first ascent on 14 July 1865 which, with its subsequent tragedy, has passed into history as one of the best known of all mountaineering stories. Zermatt's Alpine Museum is the place to visit if you have an interest in this story.

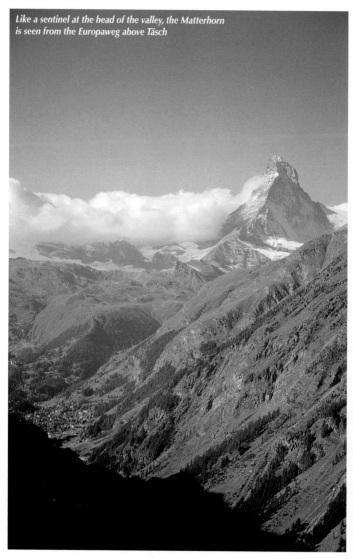

Like a sentinel at the head of the valley, the Matterhorn
is seen from the Europaweg above Täsch

About 40mins from the hut a long uphill section of fixed ropes leads to more larchwoods and a sign to the Kinhütte. Our path descends a little and shortly turns a spur to enter the **WILDIKIN** combe. It is here that the path has been engineered through a tunnel about 100m long (although there are solar-powered lights, a headtorch may be useful). Out of the tunnel a steel footbridge spans the Wildibach torrent draining the Kingletscher, then the path curves round the south side of the combe and leaves it by turning a spur, 1½hrs from the Europa Hut.

Now the Matterhorn, Klein Matterhorn and Breithorn provide a focus at the head of the valley. Ignoring another descent option to Randa, the Europaweg makes a winding descent of the west flank of the Leiterspitzen in order to avoid a rock band and an unstable scree slope. After losing about 300m of height the path then tucks under an avalanche defence system with a projecting concrete lip to deflect falling stones. A series of short corrugated iron tunnels (no torch necessary) carries the route below the slope, before entering more larchwoods at the **TÄSCHGUFER** junction (1940m, 2hrs 25mins).

A path descends from here to Täsch, while ours continues through the woods signed to Ottavan and Zermatt – watch for chamois as you wander through these woods. Rising among slopes carpeted with alpenrose and juniper the path emerges to a splendid view of the Matterhorn, then turns into the Täschbach valley, at the head of which stands the Rimpfischhorn. Eventually come down to a service road just below

TÄSCHALP (OTTAVAN 2214M, 3HRS 15MINS)

Also known as Ottavan, this hamlet lies at the junction of the Rotbach and Täschbach glens east of Täsch. There's a restaurant/*touristenlager*, an attractive little chapel, large cowsheds and a number of chalets. Upstream the Täschalpen pastures are drained by the Mellichbach stream which flows down from glaciers hanging below the Rimpfischhorn. On the hillside north of these pastures sits the Täsch Hut, with excellent views to the Schallihorn and Weisshorn, and from which a trail leads into the Rotbach glen to the north. Accessed from Täsch in the Mattertal (minibus taxis available) by a winding service road, the Täschalp has a number of charming walks.

Accommodation & refreshments at Restaurant Täschalp-Ottovan (Europaweghütte), 40 matratzenlager places, open June to mid-October (Tel 027 967 23 01, **www.europaweghuette.ch**). Täschalp would be a good place to stay if you wish to split this long final day.

High above Zermatt the trail passes through Tufteren

Walk up the road beyond the restaurant to a car park, then follow a track to a footbridge over the Täschbach stream. Cross this and turn right onto a contouring path now heading north-west with a direct view of the Schalihorn and Weisshorn on the far side of the Mattertal. Ignore alternative paths and curve round the hillside among larchwoods, eventually joining a track at a hairpin. Follow this uphill to a footpath junction where the Europaweg bears right.

As the trail progresses high above the Mattertal so Zermatt grows in extent, with the Matterhorn growing too at the head of the valley. So come to a track at the alp hamlet of **TUFTEREN** (2215m, 5hrs 15mins, refreshments) and a choice of routes to Zermatt. The signed Europaweg path descends through the hamlet and straight down to Zermatt (1hr 15mins). Other routes are also signed, while the preferred route via Sunnegga and Findeln is described below.

Bear left along the track leading to Sunnegga. On coming to a junction take the upper of two tracks signed to Findeln, and before long reach another junction just below **SUNNEGGA** (2288m, 5hrs 30mins).

The 'proper way' to conclude the Haute Route follows the continuing track and subsequent footpaths (signed) down to **FINDELN** (2051m, 5hrs 45mins, refreshments), a pretty little alp hamlet with several restaurants, a small white chapel and a classic view of the Matterhorn. Beyond this hamlet follow the Winkelmatten path, which gives good Matterhorn views almost all the way. It passes through more larchwoods, descending in long loops, crosses the Gornergrat railway and enters **WINKELMATTEN** (1672m, accommodation, refreshments), a 'suburb' of Zermatt, to which it is linked by electric bus. Turn right by the church and wander down to conclude the Chamonix to Zermatt Walker's Haute Route as you enter Zermatt. ▶

For a fast and easy descent to Zermatt take the so-called Alpen-Metro 'Sunnegga Express' – an underground funicular – whose station is just above you near another restaurant.

Zermatt

ZERMATT (1606M, 6½–7½HRS)

One of the great Alpine resorts, Zermatt's obvious success – in terms of popularity – is inextricably linked with the Matterhorn, whose noble presence overshadows the town and everything to do with it. But the Matterhorn is only one of many fine mountains visible, if not from Zermatt's crowded but traffic-free streets, certainly from the surrounding slopes. In fact there are more 4000m summits gathered round the head of the valley than are to be found anywhere else in the Alps. It is, of course, a mountaineer's Mecca, even though mainstream activists long ago turned their backs on the area and moved to larger mountains elsewhere. The appeal of the great snow and ice peaks remains as strong as ever to middle-ability mountaineers, while walkers of all persuasions will find sufficient scope here to fill every hour of a fortnight's holiday based on the town. But apart from outdoor activity and scenic splendour, Zermatt's sense of chic has as much to do with the expensive boulevards of Paris, Rome or London as it has with mountains. If you have a fortune to spend on glamorous fashion and jewellery, you might as well spend it here as in a polluted European capital. Then toast your latest accessory in champagne with the Matterhorn as a backdrop. Now that's decadent!

Accommodation, camping, restaurants, shops, banks, PTT, railway (to Visp, Brig, Geneva, etc). Tourist Office, Bahnhofplatz, 3920 Zermatt (Tel 027 966 81 00, **www.zermatt.ch**). There are more than 80 hotels listed within Zermatt itself, and many more on the outskirts. A free-phone booking facility will be found at the tourist office by the railway station. Lower-priced accommodation: Hotel Bahnhof, beds & matratzenlager, (Tel 027 967 24 06, **www.hotelbahnhof.com**); Matterhorn Hostel, matratzenlager (Tel 027 968 19 19); Jugendherberge (youth hostel, in Winkelmatten) (Tel 027 967 23 20); Le Mazot (Tel 027 966 06 06), Hotel Stockhorn (Tel 027 967 17 47). The campsite is located just north of the railway station – functional, no frills, but well used by walkers and climbers.

ALTERNATIVE STAGE 13/14
St Niklaus – Täsch – Zermatt

Start	St Niklaus (1127m)
Distance	18km
Height gain	479m
Time	4½hrs
High point	Zermatt (1606m)
Map(s)	LS 5028T Monte Rosa–Matterhorn 1:50,000
	or LS 274T Visp & 284T Mischabel 1:50,000
Transport option	Train (St Niklaus–Zermatt)
Accommodation	Mattsand (40mins) – hotel
	Herbriggen (1hr 10mins) – hotel
	Randa (2½hrs) – hotel, pension, camping
	Täsch (3½hrs) – hotels, camping
	Zermatt – hotels, youth hostel, camping

Until the Europaweg was created (see Stages 13 & 14) this was taken as the final stage of the long walk from Chamonix to Zermatt, and although it has been eclipsed by that high and challenging trail, this valley walk will still be the preferred choice for those with limited time or as a bad-weather alternative. It is something of a tease, for naturally the Matterhorn is what you hope to see, but it remains hidden until the very end.

The walk, it must be said, is by no means the most scenic of the Haute Route for it never strays far from road or railway, and views are necessarily limited by the steep valley walls. However, it is not as uninteresting as you might fear, for there are hamlets and villages along the way, as well as ancient haybarns, meadows and forests – and the river, born of glaciers and great snowfields – that offer company along much of the route. Sadly the entry into Zermatt by this route is an anti-climax, as the northern (downvalley) end of town below the railway station seems to be a permanent construction site. But at least the Matterhorn should make up for some of that.

Cross the village square below St Niklaus railway station and bear right, then left down a narrow street to the old main road. Turn right and walk upvalley almost to the outskirts of the village (about 400m), where you

ALTERNATIVE STAGE 13/14: ST NIKLAUS – ZERMATT

ST NIKLAUS
1127m

Matter Vispa

MATTSAND
1227m

MATTERTAL

HERBRIGGEN
1263m

BREITMATTEN
1280m

RANDA
1439m

continued above

continuation

RANDA
1439m

MATTERTAL

Täschbach

TÄSCH
1438m

Matter Vispa

ZERMATT
1606m

N

0 1 2 3 4 5
km

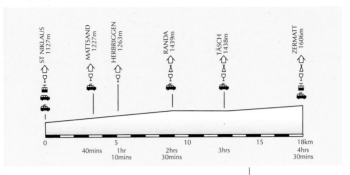

break to the right on a minor road beside Restaurant zum Frävler.

The way now follows what is apparently the 'old' road through the valley, bringing you alongside the railway line and passing some typical old Valaisian houses, as well as more modern buildings based on traditional architectural styles. In 20mins come to a group of old buildings and a small chapel; this is **ZE SCHWIDERNU** (1163m). A few mins later, as you cross the Blattbach stream which pours from the right, the Topali Hut can be seen as a silver box perched on a cliff 1400m above. In 40mins arrive in

> **MATTSAND** (1227m, 40mins) Accommodation at Hotel zum Frävler (Tel 027 956 27 07, **www. fraevler.ch**).

Still on the old road cross back over the railway line and the river beyond to gain a fine view of the Breithorn upvalley. The road now skirts a large settlement reservoir, and when the tarmac road bears left round the southern end, go directly ahead on a continuing track. About 1min along this track pass a small picnic area on the left, and on the right a view up to a series of cascades pouring through the Tummigbach gorge. Shortly after this emerge from a wooded area to open meadows and old haybarns, the village of Herbriggen across the river, and another lovely view of the Breithorn.

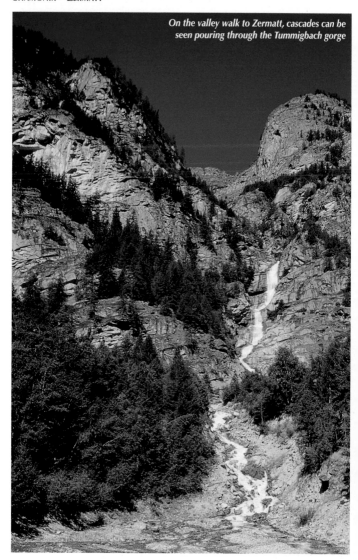

*On the valley walk to Zermatt, cascades can be
seen pouring through the Tummigbach gorge*

THE BREITHORN

A near neighbour of the Matterhorn, the Breithorn is a massive snow and ice mountain of 4164m, with a 3km-long summit ridge. By its standard route (the SSW Flank) it is said to be one of the easiest of the alpine 4000ers to climb. But it also has some difficult and dangerous lines, especially on the North Face. It was first climbed (by today's *voie normale*) in 1813.

At the far end of the meadow the track forks, with the left branch crossing the river to HERBRIGGEN (accommodation, refreshments). Continue upvalley along the right-hand side of the Mattervispa river, and in 1hr 10mins come to a footbridge crossing the river to Herbriggen station. Again, do not cross, but remain on the west side of the river on a footpath signed to Randa, Täsch and Zermatt.

The path briefly accompanies the Mattervispa, then climbs among trees and forks. Keep ahead over a footbridge and contour briefly alongside a *bisse* before climbing again, twisting uphill through mixed woodland. Having gained a high point, you then descend to the river and cross by footbridge. Go up a slope for a few paces, then bear right on a track signed to Randa. Just ahead can be seen the results of a massive rockfall.

In April 1991 a huge **rockfall** reshaped the mountainside north-west of Randa when a vast section of the Langenflueberg collapsed into the valley, demolishing the railway, blocking the river and cutting off the upper Mattertal for several days. Hundreds of large boulders still litter the valley where they came to rest in the meadows – close to chalets and haybarns – just below Randa.

Keeping company with the river the track continues upstream, then brings you to a service road by a bridge. Walk up the road. Screened from the river by a line of larch trees, the road rises gently. When it forks continue ahead, but on coming to some haybarns leave the road for a track cutting ahead to the right (1hr 55mins), with views now of the Weisshorn, with the icefall of the Bisgletscher just below it.

About 10mins along the track come to a road by a bridge on the outskirts of **RANDA** (accommodation, refreshments, camping, trains to Zermatt). Cross the bridge and turn left on a riverside footpath which brings you to another junction 5mins later. Remain on the treelined riverside path, which after a while rises through forest, then descends again to the river and forks. Cross the river to another service road, recross the river once more, then continue on the riverside path. This goes up a brief slope, passes a shrine and leads to the Matterhorn Golf Course.

RANDA

Situated in the valley midway between the Weisshorn and the Dom, the attractive village of Randa is developing into a low-key alternative to Zermatt. It stands above the main Mattertal road and railway, so is relieved of through-traffic pressure. From the village a steep path climbs to the Europa Hut in 2¼hrs (see Stage 13) and the higher Dom Hut in 4hrs. On the other side of the valley a 4¼hr walk leads to the Weisshorn Hut. Apart from these lofty destinations, there are other good walks to be tackled from this valley base. The campsite, just to the south of Randa, has excellent facilities and views of the Zinalrothorn.

Skirt the right-hand side of the golf course, partly weaving through woodland, and eventually come to a group of buildings and a track. The track winds round a large building, continues upvalley a short distance, then twists left to cross a side stream. Turn left on the continuing track, which soon curves to the right and goes alongside a man-made lake, at the far end of which you come to a large car- and coach-park.

Cross the car park to an access road and resume alongside the Mattervispa river, soon passing a picnic area with a water supply on the right. In 3hrs come to Camping Alphubel opposite **TÄSCH** (1438m accommodation, refreshments, shops, bank, PTT, trains to Zermatt). A bridge crosses the river to the village, but again, as with Randa, it is not necessary to cross unless you need its facilities. Instead, remain on the west bank of the river and 20mins from the campsite you reach a group of barns where the way divides.

Täschalp, on the final stage of the walk to Zermatt

TÄSCH

Noted for the monstrous car parks which fill the meadows to the north of the railway station, Täsch is where the great majority of motoring visitors to Zermatt leave their vehicles before catching the train for the final leg of the journey upvalley. (Motor vehicles are banned from Zermatt.) The village that most people see is so dominated by this traffic that it has little identity of its own – almost everything here leans towards Zermatt. However, the original village stands aloof from all this on the west side of the valley, and is much more attractive and typically Valaisian in its architecture. Behind it a steeply twisting service road climbs the hillside and enters the lovely, unspoilt Täschbach glen in which lies the hamlet of Täschalp, and above which stands the Täsch Hut. There are some peaceful and scenic walks to be had up there, including sections of the Europaweg adopted by Stage 14.

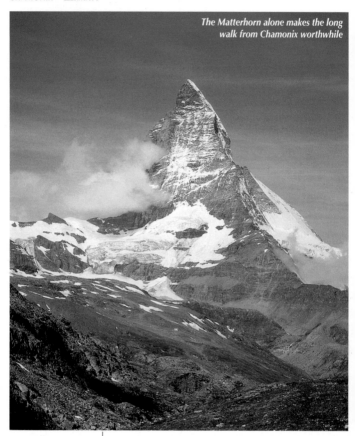

The Matterhorn alone makes the long walk from Chamonix worthwhile

Reluctant to finish the walk on our first Haute Route trek we sat on a bench on the outskirts of Zermatt. Since first light we'd had rain and knee-high clouds which somehow helped counter-balance all the fine-weather days. If views were to be denied us, this was definitely the day for it. Of course, that meant no Matterhorn, but what we had experienced in the previous two weeks more than made up for that loss. At Täsch the rain had stopped, but low clouds still obscured every view. Seated on the damp bench outside Zermatt we reviewed the walk as a whole, and concluded that it had been one of the most beautiful either of us had ever undertaken. (Between us we had more than 50 years of mountain experience.) Without doubt we'd be back to walk it again (as we have, several times). But for now we were in no hurry for it to be over. For all its undeniable attractions and for all its being the culmination of the walk that had begun on a sunny afternoon in Chamonix, Zermatt was not going to be another of those quiet, unassuming hamlets that had added so much to the route. We were about to face the crowds – and that would be a culture shock. So we sat among the clouds and put off the final ten-minute stroll into town. And we'd still be sitting there now had the rain not started once more.

Next day we were blessed with blue skies and sunshine, and so wandered upvalley with eyes transfixed by the sight of that great pyramid of rock. Our pilgrimage from Chamonix to Zermatt – Mont Blanc to the Matterhorn – was complete.

Bear right on a path which climbs among larch-woods. A sign in a clearing gives 40mins to Zermatt, and in a little over 4hrs come to a high point to see the Matterhorn ahead for the first time, with Zermatt below.

ZERMATT (1606M, 4½HRS)

As one of the great Alpine resorts Zermatt has no real closed season. It's busy throughout the year – if not with skiers, walkers or climbers, then with the crowds of general tourists who flock there either to pay homage to the Matterhorn or to add the town to the tick-list of European hot-spots. Zermatt has something for everyone, and it's impossible to be bored there. If you don't like the crowds, there are paths that lead to magnificent viewpoints where even in the height of summer you can experience true solitude, and no shortage of other trails that, while not being empty, are well worth taking for their variety and extravagant panoramas. (See Appendix A for a sample.) If you're stuck in town on a wet day, why not visit the interesting Alpine Museum near the post office?

Accommodation, camping, restaurants, shops, banks, PTT, railway (to Visp, Brig, Geneva, etc). Tourist Office, Bahnhofplatz, 3920 Zermatt (Tel 027 966 81 00, **www.zermatt.ch**). For full accommodation information see the end of Stage 14.

APPENDIX A
Route summary table

Stage		Distance	Height gain	Time	Page
1	Chamonix–Argentière	9km	214m	2hrs	40
2	Argentière–Col de Balme–Trient	12km	953m	5–5½hrs	46
Alt 2	Argentière–Col de Balme–Les Grands– Col de la Forclaz	15km	953m	6½–7hrs	54
3	Trient–Fenêtre d'Arpette–Champex	14km	1386m	6½–7hrs	58
Alt 3	Trient–Col de la Forclaz–Bovine–Champex	16km	929m	5½hrs	66
4	Champex–Sembrancher–Le Châble	13km	104m	3½–4hrs	70
5	Le Châble–Clambin–Cabane du Mont Fort	9km	1636m	6–6½hrs	77
6	Cab. du Mont Fort–Col de Louvie–Col de Prafleuri–Cab. de Prafleuri	14km	885m	6–6½hrs	85
Alt 6	Cab. du Mont Fort–Col de la Chaux– Col de Prafleuri–Cab. de Prafleuri	10km	885m	5½hrs	92
7	Cab. de Prafleuri–Col des Roux–Col de Riedmatten–Arolla	16km	735m	6½hrs	95
Alt 7	Cab. de Prafleuri–Col des Roux–Cab. des Dix – Arolla	17km	837m	6½hrs	105
8	Arolla–Lac Bleu–Les Haudères–La Sage	10km	215m	4hrs	110
9	La Sage–Col du Tsaté–Cabane de Moiry	10km	1617m	5–5½hrs	118
Alt 9	La Sage–Col de Torrent–Barrage de Moiry	10km	1252m	5hrs	125
10	Cabane de Moiry–Col de Sorebois–Zinal	14km	462m	5–5½hrs	131

Stage		Distance	Height gain	Time	Page
Alt 10	Barrage de Moiry–Col de Sorebois–Zinal	8km	598m	4–4½hrs	136
11	Zinal–Forcletta–Gruben	14km	1199m	5½–6hrs	138
Alt 11	Zinal–Hotel Weisshorn/ Cabane Bella Tola	10km	725m	3½–4hrs	146
Alt 11A	Hotel Weisshorn/Cabane Bella Tola– Meidpass –Gruben	9km	589m	4hrs	153
12	Gruben–Augstbordpass– St Niklaus	16km	1072m	6½–7hrs	159
12A	St Niklaus–Gasenried	4km	532m	1½–2hrs	170
13	Gasenried–Europa Hut	14km	1131m	5½–6½hrs	176
14	Europa Hut–Täschalp–Zermatt	18km	348m	6½–7hrs	185
Alt 13/14	St Niklaus–Täsch–Zermatt	18km	479m	4½hrs	193

The old Valaisian hamlet of Zum See, a short walk from Zermatt's bustling streets

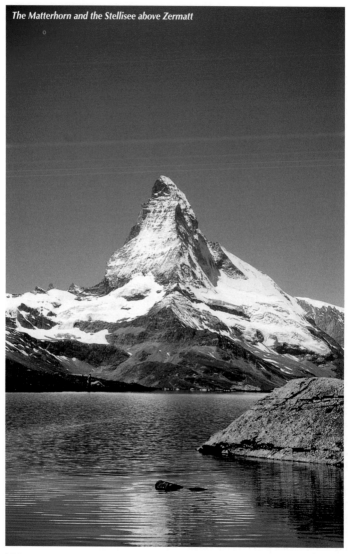

The Matterhorn and the Stellisee above Zermatt

APPENDIX B

Walks from Zermatt

Should you have a day or two in hand on arrival in Zermatt and want to make the most of your time there, the handful of walks outlined below will provide some ideas. It is just a brief sample from the many to be had, but each one has its own special attributes and is highly recommended. Other ideas may be gleaned from the regional guidebook *Walking in the Valais* (published by Cicerone Press), which is readily available in the UK and is also usually on sale in Zermatt's main bookshop.

The Schönbiel Hut

This is one of the finest of all walks in the area giving a full day's outing – there and back. The path leads upvalley to Zmutt and beyond in full view of the Matterhorn. It takes you across glacial streams and along a moraine crest to the hut which is situated on a grassy bluff south-west of Zermatt, at 2694m, and with superb views onto a world of ice dominated by Dent d'Hérens and the Matterhorn. (4hrs and 11km to the hut. Allow 6½hrs for the round trip.)

Trift & Hobalmen

The first part of this walk climbs through the confines of the Trift gorge immediately west of Zermatt, emerging to views of a glacier-hung cirque from the Victorian Hotel du Trift. From here you face several choices, but for the renowned belvedere viewpoint of Höhbalmen (2665m) a path is taken which crosses the Triftbach to the south and rises over grass slopes to turn a shoulder, beyond which you come to a wonderful broad pastureland with a great sweep of mountains and glaciers in view. At a junction of paths you can either descend to Zermatt via the alp huts of Hubel and Herbrigg (a 4hr walk), or remain high on the continuing path that eventually descends into the Arben glen to join the Schönbiel Hut path (see the Schönbiel Hut walk, above). Bear left and return to Zermatt via Zmutt for a 7hr walk.

The Hornli Hut

Situated at 3260m at the foot of the steep ridge on the Matterhorn from which it takes its name, the Hörnli Hut is where most climbers spend the night before embarking on the standard route to the summit. The hut enjoys a truly dramatic position overlooking a highway of ice leading to Monte Rosa. The walk from Zermatt is an extremely steep one (4½–5hrs), although the effort can be greatly reduced by taking the cable-car to Schwarzsee and beginning the walk there (2hrs to the hut).

The Monte Rosa Hut

Here's a glacier walk with exciting views – but it should only be attempted by walkers experienced in crossing crevassed icefields! Alternatively, simply walk as far as the glacier edge, then return to Zermatt via Riffelsee and Riffelalp (6hrs in all). First take the Gornergrat railway as far as Rotenboden (try to get a seat on the right-hand side of the carriage for the best views), and on leaving the train descend a little towards the much-photographed Riffelsee, then cross a low ridge on the left. A good path cuts across the south flank of the Gornergrat ridge (*grat* actually means 'ridge') above the Gorner glacier, from which you gaze directly at that huge ice wall of Monte Rosa, Liskamm, Castor, Pollux and Breithorn which forms the Swiss–Italian border. The path leads to the glacier edge, and the route across the ice is usually marked: do not stray from the marked route for there are many crevasses; great care is needed. All safety precautions should be taken. Once across the glacier the way scrambles up bands of rock to gain the hut in about 2½hrs.

From the Monte Rosa Hut one looks along the Gorner glacier to the distant Matterhorn – a truly memorable sight. (Allow 2–2½hrs back to Rotenboden, or 5–5½hrs to walk all the way to Zermatt.)

Fluhalp & four mountain tarns

For a less demanding day than any of the above walks, ride the underground funicular to Sunnegga at 2288m, descend a little, then take a signed path beyond the little Leisee tarn heading roughly east to the Stellisee and continue to the Berghütte Fluhalp (2607m), which is backed by moraines of the Findel glacier. Leaving the inn go down a track to a path serving the little Grindjisee, then continue by scenic track and footpath to the Grüensee. A short distance beyond this tarn stands the Bärghaus Grüensee near a path junction. The right-hand trail goes down to a footbridge over the Findelbach stream. Either walk down the left bank of the stream or cross over to the lovely alp hamlet of Findeln (visited on the final stage of the Europaweg) and descend from there to Zermatt (a 4½hr walk).

APPENDIX C
Climbing from Zermatt

Given time at the end of the Chamonix to Zermatt trek, and taking advantage of fitness, seasoned mountain walkers may be tempted to round off their trip by making the ascent of one of Zermatt's surrounding peaks. The Matterhorn is an obvious choice, but there are plenty of others. Experienced alpinists will need no advice from this book, but are directed to the two Alpine Club guidebooks to the area: *Valais Alps East* by Les Swindin & Peter Fleming, and *Valais Alps West* by Lindsay Griffin. The following notes, however, may be helpful for those with experience of climbing in Britain, but whose first visit to the Alps this is.

The first thing to understand is the scale of these mountains. After two weeks of wandering across their lower ridges you will have some idea of just how big they are, but it is only by setting out to climb them that the full stature of alpine mountains can be properly appreciated. They should never be underestimated. Unless you have a member of your party with all-round experience of climbing in the Alps, who is competent to lead a climb or two from here, my advice is to leave well alone or hire a professional guide.

Zermatt has its own mountain guide's office (the *Alpin Center*) with 50 or more official guides working from it. The office is found on the main street south of the railway station (www.zermatt.ch/alpincenter). Guided excursions suitable for beginners are arranged daily, weather permitting. These include a 4hr glacier trek from the Klein Matterhorn to Trockener Steg, basic climbing instruction on the Riffelhorn, or the ascent of such 4000m peaks as the Allalinhorn and Weissmies.

A variety of other peaks can be offered, but it should be stressed that to employ a professional mountain guide here can be very expensive – although that expense may be justified by the knowledge that the experience of standing on top of your first alpine peak is likely to be one you'll always remember.

The cost of employing a guide for the climb itself is only part of the expense. Add to this the guide's food in a mountain hut (an overnight is usually necessary), hut fees for yourself and the guide, and hire of equipment – you'll no doubt need crampons, plus ice-axe – which can be rented from one of the many local sports shops. (The guide provides the rope.) It is also necessary to have mountain accident and rescue insurance.

The Mettelhorn
At 3406m this modest peak is not in the same league as those mentioned below, but is a popular 'tourist' summit

because of the extent and richness of its panorama. In times past an ascent of the Mettelhorn formed part of the training programme of mountaineers newly arrived in the area, for the 1800m difference in height from Zermatt to summit was considered ideal for acclimatisation and testing one's fitness! Having spent two weeks walking from Chamonix you ought to be fit by now, and the 6hr ascent by way of the Trift gorge, involving no technical difficulty, should be within the capabilities of most C–Z trekkers.

The Breithorn

Generally considered the easiest of the local 4000m summits (and possibly the easiest for its height in the Alps), the 4164m Breithorn is situated midway between Monte Rosa and the Matterhorn. The summit is reached from the Gandegg Hut via the Theodule Pass in about 4hrs, while a shorter (1½hr) ascent of the SSW flank is often tackled from the Klein Matterhorn, graded PD-. The Breithorn is an extremely popular mountain, but given the serious nature of crevassed areas and the difficulties of route-finding in poor visibility, it should never be underestimated.

The Matterhorn

At 4477m this is possibly the one alpine peak all attracted to mountains would love to climb. The standard route by way of the Hörnli ridge is not difficult by alpine standards, but is nevertheless a serious undertaking for novices, the rock being loose and downright dangerous in places. (The route is graded AD-, with numerous individual grade II and III rock pitches.) One of the problems faced by climbers on this route is salvos of stonefall; another, general to this mountain, is the bad weather it attracts. From the Hörnli Hut an average time to the summit for experienced climbers would be 5–6hrs.

Monte Rosa

Containing the second highest summit in the Alps (the 4634m Dufourspitze) the Monte Rosa massif, which has no less than ten 4000m tops, is the largest mountain mass in Western Europe. Shared between Switzerland and Italy this beautiful snow- and ice-bound mountain boasts a number of lengthy routes. From the Monte Rosa Hut (see Appendix A) the Dufourspitze may be tackled by a popular snow climb up its north-west flank and then along the west ridge in 6–7hrs (PD, II+ 40°). The first ascent was achieved in August 1855.

There are, of course, numerous other peaks in the area, many of which have routes of greater interest or challenge to experienced climbers. In addition there are glacier tours that would provide memorable days out. You need never run short of ideas in Zermatt.

APPENDIX D
Useful Addresses

Tourist Information
Switzerland Travel Centre Ltd
30 Bedford Street
London WC2E 9ED
Tel 00800 100 200 29
info.uk@myswitzerland.com
www.myswitzerland.com

British Mountaineering Council
177–179 Burton Road
Manchester M20 2BB
Tel 0161 445 6111
office@thebmc.co.uk
www.thebmc.co.uk

Switzerland Tourism
608 Fifth Avenue
New York
NY 10020
Tel 011800-100 200 30
info.usa@myswitzerland.com

Club Alpin Suisse
Monbijoustr. 61
3000 Bern 23
Tel 031 370 18 18
info@sac-cas.ch
www.sac-cas.ch

Map Suppliers
Swiss topographical maps can also be ordered online from the Federal Office of Topography in Switzerland via www.swisstopo.ch

Edward Stanford Ltd
12–14 Long Acre
London WC2E 9LP
Tel 0207 836 1321
sales@stanfords.co.uk
www.stanfords.co.uk

The Map Shop
15 High Street
Upton-upon-Severn
Worcs WR8 0HJ
Tel 0800 085 4080 (UK only)
Tel 01684 593146
themapshop@btinternet.com
www.themapshop.co.uk

Cordee Ltd
Tel 01455 611185
www.cordee.co.uk

Zermatt, journey's end

Specialist Mountain Activities Insurance
BMC Travel & Activity Insurance
(BMC members only)
177–179 Burton Road
Manchester M20 2BB
Tel 0161 445 6111
www.thebmc.co.uk

Austrian Alpine Club
12a North Street
Wareham
Dorset BH20 4AG
Tel 01929 556 870
aac.office@aacuk.org.uk
aacuk.org.uk

*Membership of the AAC carries
accident & mountain rescue insurance
plus reciprocal-rights reductions in
SAC huts.*

Snowcard Insurance Services
Lower Boddington
Daventry
Northants NN11 6XZ
Tel 0844 826 2699
assistance@snowcard.co.uk
www.snowcard.co.uk

Harrison Beaumont Ltd
2 Des Roches Square
Witney
Oxon OX8 6BE
Tel 01993 700 200
info@hbinsurance.co.uk
www.hbinsurance.co.uk

APPENDIX E
Bibliography

General Tourist Guides

The Rough Guide to Switzerland by Matthew Teller (Rough Guides, 4th edition 2010) – Of the many general tourist guides on the market, this is the best and most comprehensive. Entertaining, factual, full of surprises and highly recommended.

Switzerland by Damien Simonis, Sarah Johnstone & Lorne Jackson (Lonely Planet, 4th edition 2003) – Good coverage, in typical Lonely Planet style.

Blue Guide to Switzerland by Ian Robertson (A&C Black) – Regularly updated and worth consulting.

Michelin Tourist Guide – French Alps (Michelin, 1998) – Useful information for visitors to the Chamonix–Mont Blanc region.

The Green Guide to Switzerland (Michelin, 2000)

The Alps by RLG Irving (Batsford, 1939) – Long out of print, but available on special request from public libraries (it may also be obtainable via internet booksearch sites), this book contains lengthy chapters on both the Mont Blanc range and that of the Pennine Alps, with some interesting background information.

Mountains and Mountaineering

Numerous volumes devoted to mountaineering in regions of the Alps through which the Chamonix–Zermatt route travels are to be found in bookshops and libraries. Those listed below represent a very small selection, but there should be plenty of reading to provide an appetizer for a forthcoming visit – or to feed nostalgia.

The High Mountains of the Alps by Helmut Dumler and Willi P Burkhardt (Diadem Books, London/The Mountaineers, Seattle 1994) – A sumptuous large format book devoted to all the alpine 4000m peaks, of which there are many along the Haute Route. Mouth-watering photography and intelligent text make this a collector's item.

Alps 4000 by Martin Moran (David & Charles, 1994) – This is the fascinating account of Moran's and Simon Jenkins's epic journey across all the 4000 metre summits of the Alps in one summer's frenetic activity.

Scrambles Amongst the Alps by Edward Whymper (first edition 1871, numerous editions since, including one published in 1986 by Webb & Bower, with superb colour photos by John Cleare) – Scrambles is the classic volume of mountaineering literature which covers Whymper's alpine campaigns from 1860 to 1865. It contains the account of his fateful first ascent of the Matterhorn, but much more besides of interest to walkers of the Haute Route.

Wanderings Among the High Alps by Alfred Wills (Blackwell – latest edition 1937) – Another record of Victorian adventures with guides on peaks and passes of the Pennine Alps, as well as other areas.

The Alps in 1864 by AW Moore (Blackwell – latest edition 1939) – A two-volume personal account of a summer's mountaineering with Whymper and Horace Walker.

On High Hills by Geoffrey Winthrop Young (Methuen, 1927) – Winthrop Young was one of the great pre-First World War climbers whose accounts are of high literary merit. This volume includes many references to the Pennine Alps.

Men and the Matterhorn by Gaston Rébuffet (Kaye & Ward, 1973) – A well-illustrated book dedicated to the most famous mountain in Europe.

The Mountains of Switzerland by Herbert Maeder (George Allen & Unwin, 1968) – Large format book with magnificent monochrome photographs.

Alpine Points of View by Kev Reynolds (Cicerone Press, 2004) – 101 full-page colour photographs, plus evocative text, that depicts the diverse landscapes of the alpine range – includes a number of images taken on the Walker's Haute Route.

The Outdoor Traveler's Guide to The Alps by Marcia R Lieberman (Stewart, Tabori & Chang, New York 1991) – Much of the range is covered, albeit in brief essays, but Mont Blanc and several of the Pennine valleys are treated well. The book is illustrated by Tim Thompson's high-quality colour photographs.

Alpine Ski Tour by Robin Fedden (Putnam, 1956) – An account of the High Level Route ski traverse.

Mountain Walking

Walking in the Valais by Kev Reynolds (Cicerone Press, 4th edition 2014) – A walking guide in the same series as the present book, it covers all the valleys of

the Pennine Alps traversed on this route; 120 walks described.

Mont Blanc Walks by Hilary Sharp (Cicerone Press, 2005) – A selection of 50 walks and four multi-day treks in the shadow of Mont Blanc by a respected guidebook writer and trekking guide.

Tour of Mont Blanc by Kev Reynolds (Cicerone Press, 4th Edition 2015) – The early stages of the C–Z trek are shared by the TMB. This is the standard guide to that classic trek.

100 Hut Walks in the Alps by Kev Reynolds (Cicerone Press, 3rd edition 2014) – As the title suggests, a large selection of alpine hut walks. Some of those used on the Chamonix–Zermatt route are included.

Classic Walks in the Alps by Kev Reynolds (Oxford Illustrated Press, 1991) – A large format book which describes, among others, the Chamonix–Zermatt route plus several day walks in the Pennine Alps.

Tour of the Matterhorn by Hilary Sharp (Cicerone Press, 2006) – A guide to this 'new' circular trek which shares several stages of the C–Z route, but in the opposite direction.

Trekking in the Alps edited by Kev Reynolds (Cicerone Press, 2012) – The Chamonix to Zermatt route is included in a selection of the 20 best Alpine treks.

The Swiss Alps by Kev Reynolds (Cicerone Press, 2011) – A resource for independent adventurers planning to walk, trek or climb here, described in detail valley by valley.

Walking in the Alps by Kev Reynolds (Cicerone Press, 2nd edition, 2005) – From the Alpes Maritime to the Julians of Slovenia, 19 regions of the Alps are described with their walking and trekking potential in this 495 page alpine 'bible'. The Pennine Alps and Mont Blanc range are well covered.

Walking in the Alps by J Hubert Walker (Oliver & Boyd, 1951) – Inspiration for the previous title, Walker's book has long been out of print. Although much has changed in the Alps since it was written, it remains one of the best and most readable of all alpine books. A fine chapter is devoted to the Pennine Alps.

Walking in the Alps by Helen Fairbairn, Gareth McCormack, Sandra Bardwell, Grant Dixon and Clem Lindenmayer (Lonely Planet, 2004) – A selection of multi-day tours and treks, includes the Walker's Haute Route.

Walking in Switzerland by Clem Lindenmayer (Lonely Planet, 2nd edition 2001) – Good coverage of most Swiss mountain regions, in the Lonely Planet format.

Backpacking in the Alps and Pyrenees by Showell Styles (Gollancz, 1976) – Contains an account of a large section of the Walker's Haute Route.

The Walker's Haute Route by Alexander Stewart (Trailblazer, 2008) – A recently-published guide which follows the same route as the present book, but in Trailblazer style.

Climbing and Ski-touring Guides

Valais Alps East by Les Swindin and Peter Fleming (Alpine Club, 1999) – A 'selected climbs' guidebook which includes many of the summits above Zermatt, but not the Matterhorn.

Valais Alps West by Lindsay Griffin (Alpine Club, 1998) – Produced by that doyen of mountaineering journalists, this is the companion volume to the guide above. It covers most high peaks of the Pennine Alps from the Mont Vélan group to the Matterhorn.

The Haute Route Chamonix–Zermatt by Peter Cliff (Cordee) – Describes the glacier route for ski-tourers.

Alpine Ski Mountaineering: Volume 1 – Western Alps by Bill O'Connor (Cicerone Press, 2003) – An inspirational guidebook to a number of terrific ski tours, it includes the Classic Haute Route, plus others in the Pennine Alps.

APPENDIX F
Glossary

The following glossary is a selection of words likely to be found on maps, in village streets or in foreign-language tourist information leaflets. It is no substitute for a pocket dictionary, but hopefully will be of some practical use.

German	French	English
Abhang	pente	slope
Alp	haut pâturage	alp
Alpenblume	florealpe	alpine flower
Alpenverein	club alpin	alpine club
Alphütte	cabane, refuge	mountain hut
Auskunft	renseignements	information
Aussichtspunkt	belle vue	viewpoint
Bach	ruisseau	stream, river
Bäckerei	boulangerie	bakery
Bahnhof	la gare	railway station
Berg	montagne	mountain
Bergführer	guide de montagne	mountain guide
Berggasthaus	hotel en haut	mountain inn
Bergpass	col	pass
Bergschrund	rimaye	crevasse between glacier and rock wall
Bergsteiger	alpiniste	mountaineer
Bergwanderer	grimpeur	hillwalker
Bergweg	chemin de montagne	mountain path
Blatt	feuille	map sheet
Brücke	pont	bridge
Dorf	village	village
Drahtseilbahn	télépherique	cable-car

German	French	English
Ebene	*plaine or plan*	plain
Fels	*rocher*	rock wall
Ferienwohnung	*apartement de vacances*	holiday apartment
Fussweg	*sentier, chemin*	footpath
Garni	*garni*	b&b hotel
Gasthaus or gasthof	*auberge*	inn, guest house
Gaststube	*salon*	common room
Gefährlich	*dangereaux*	dangerous
Gemse	*chamois*	chamois
Geröllhalde	*éboulis*	scree
Gipfel	*sommet, cime*	summit, peak
Gletscher	*glacier*	glacier
Gletscherspalte	*crevasse*	crevasse
Gondelbahn	*télécabin*	gondola lift
Grat	*arête*	ridge
Grüetzi	*bonjour*	greetings
Jugendherberge	*auberge de jeunesse*	youth hostel
Kamm	*crête*	crest, ridge
Kapelle	*chapelle*	chapel
Karte	*carte*	map
Kirche	*église*	church
Klamm	*gorge,*	ravin
Klumme	*combe*	combe, small valley
Landschaft	*paysage*	landscape
Lawine	*avalanche*	avalanche
Lebensmittel	*épicerie*	grocery
Leicht	*facile*	easy
Links	*á gauche*	left (direction)

German	French	English
Matratzenlager/ massenlager	dortoir	dormitory
Moräne	moraine	moraine
Murmeltier	marmot	marmot
Nebel	brouillard	fog, low cloud, mist
Nord	nord	north
Ober	dessus	upper
Ost	est	east
Pass	col	pass
Pension	pension	simple hotel
Pfad	sentier, chemin	path
Pickel	piolet	ice-axe
Quelle	source, fontaine	spring
Rechts	á droite	right (direction)
Reh	chevreuil	roe deer
Rucksack	sac à dos	rucksack
Sattel	selle	saddle, pass
Schlafraum	dortoir, chambre	bedroom
Schlafsaal	dortoir	dormitory
Schloss	château	castle
Schlucht	ravin, gorge	gorge
Schnee	neige	snow
See	lac	lake, tarn
Seil	corde	rope
Seilbahn	télépherique	cable-car
Sesselbahn	télésèige	chairlift
Stausee	réservoir	reservoir
Steigesen	crampons	crampons
Steinmann	cairn	cairn

German	French	English
Steinschlag	*chute de pierres*	stonefall
Stunde(n)	*heure(s)*	hour(s)
Sud	*sud*	south
Tal	*vallée*	valley
Tobel	*ravin boisé*	wooded ravine
Touristenlager	*dortoir*	dormitory, simple accommodation
Über	*via, par-dessus*	via, or over
Unfall	*accident*	accident
Unterkunft	*logement*	accommodation
Verkehrsverein	*office du tourisme*	tourist office
Wald	*forêt, bois*	forest
Wanderweg	*sentier, chemin*	footpath
Wasser	*eau*	water
Weide	*pâturage*	pasture
West	*ouest*	west
Wildbach	*torrent*	torrent
Zeltplatz	*camping*	campsite
Zimmer	*chambres*	bedrooms
– frei		– vacancies

NOTES

Walking – Trekking – Mountaineering – Climbing – Cycling

Over 40 years, Cicerone have built up an outstanding collection of 300 guides, inspiring all sorts of amazing adventures.

Every guide comes from extensive exploration and research by our expert authors, all with a passion for their subjects. They are frequently praised, endorsed and used by clubs, instructors and outdoor organisations.

All our titles can now be bought as **e-books** and many as iPad and Kindle files and we will continue to make all our guides available for these and many other devices.

Our website shows any **new information** we've received since a book was published. Please do let us know if you find anything has changed, so that we can pass on the latest details. On our **website** you'll also find some great ideas and lots of information, including sample chapters, contents lists, reviews, articles and a photo gallery.

It's easy to keep in touch with what's going on at Cicerone, by getting our monthly **free e-newsletter**, which is full of offers, competitions, up-to-date information and topical articles. You can subscribe on our home page and also follow us on **Facebook** and **Twitter**, as well as our **blog**.

Cicerone – the very best guides for exploring the world.

CICERONE

2 Police Square Milnthorpe Cumbria LA7 7PY
Tel: 015395 62069 info@cicerone.co.uk
www.cicerone.co.uk

Walking in Corsica
Walking in Provence – East
Walking in Provence – West
Walking in the Auvergne
Walking in the Cevennes
Walking in the Dordogne
Walking in the Haute Savoie –
    North & South
Walking in the Languedoc
Walking in the Tarentaise and
    Beaufortain Alps
Walks in the Cathar Region

GERMANY

Germany's Romantic Road
Hiking and Biking in the
    Black Forest
Walking in the Bavarian Alps

HIMALAYA

Annapurna
Bhutan
Everest
Garhwal and Kumaon
Langtang with Gosainkund
    and Helambu
Manaslu
The Mount Kailash Trek
Trekking in Ladakh
Trekking in the Himalaya

ICELAND & GREENLAND

Trekking in Greenland
Walking and Trekking in Iceland

IRELAND

Irish Coastal Walks
The Irish Coast to Coast Walk
The Mountains of Ireland

ITALY

Gran Paradiso
Sibillini National Park
Shorter Walks in the Dolomites
Through the Italian Alps
Trekking in the Apennines
Trekking in the Dolomites
Via Ferratas of the Italian
    Dolomites: Vols 1 & 2
Walking in Abruzzo
Walking in Italy's Stelvio
    National Park
Walking in Sardinia
Walking in Sicily
Walking in the Central
    Italian Alps

Walking in the Dolomites
Walking in Tuscany
Walking in Umbria
Walking on the Amalfi Coast
Walking the Italian Lakes

MEDITERRANEAN

Jordan – Walks, Treks, Caves,
    Climbs and Canyons
The Ala Dag
The High Mountains of Crete
The Mountains of Greece
Treks and Climbs in Wadi Rum
Walking in Malta
Western Crete

NORTH AMERICA

British Columbia
The Grand Canyon
The John Muir Trail
The Pacific Crest Trail

SOUTH AMERICA

Aconcagua and the
    Southern Andes
Hiking and Biking Peru's
    Inca Trails
Torres del Paine

SCANDINAVIA

Walking in Norway

SLOVENIA, CROATIA AND MONTENEGRO

The Islands of Croatia
The Julian Alps of Slovenia
The Mountains of Montenegro
Trekking in Slovenia
Walking in Croatia
Walking in Slovenia: The
    Karavanke

SPAIN AND PORTUGAL

Costa Blanca: West
Mountain Walking in
    Southern Catalunya
The Mountains of Central Spain
The Mountains of Nerja
The Northern Caminos
Trekking through Mallorca
Walking in Madeira
Walking in Mallorca
Walking in Menorca
Walking in the Algarve
Walking in the Cordillera
    Cantabrica

Walking in the Sierra Nevada
Walking on Gran Canaria
Walking on La Gomera and
    El Hierro
Walking on La Palma
Walking on Lanzarote and
    Fuerteventura
Walking on Tenerife
Walking the GR7 in Andalucia
Walks and Climbs in the
    Picos de Europa

SWITZERLAND

Alpine Pass Route
Central Switzerland
The Bernese Alps
The Swiss Alps
Tour of the Jungfrau Region
Walking in the Valais
Walking in Ticino
Walks in the Engadine

TECHNIQUES

Geocaching in the UK
Indoor Climbing
Lightweight Camping
Map and Compass
Mountain Weather
Moveable Feasts
Outdoor Photography
Polar Exploration
Rock Climbing
Sport Climbing
The Book of the Bivvy
The Hillwalker's Guide to
    Mountaineering
The Hillwalker's Manual

MINI GUIDES

Alpine Flowers
Avalanche!
Navigating with a GPS
Navigation
Pocket First Aid and
    Wilderness Medicine
Snow

MOUNTAIN LITERATURE

8000 metres
A Walk in the Clouds
Unjustifiable Risk?

For full information on all our
guides, books and eBooks,
visit our website:
www.cicerone.co.uk.

LISTING OF CICERONE GUIDES